Epworth Commen

General Editor
Ivor H. Jones

The Epistle to the Romans

The Epistle to the
ROMANS

KENNETH GRAYSTON

EPWORTH PRESS

0 7162 0511 4

First Published 1997
by Epworth Press
20 Ivatt Way
Peterborough, PE3 7PG

Typeset by Regent Typesetting, London
Printed and bound in Great Britain by
Biddles Ltd, Guildford and King's Lynn

CONTENTS

GENERAL INTRODUCTION

The *Epworth Preachers' Commentaries* that Greville P. Lewis edited so successfully in the 1950s and 1960s having now served their turn, the Epworth Press has commissioned a team of distinguished academics who are also preachers and teachers to create a new series of commentaries that will serve the 1990s and beyond. We have seized the opportunity offered by the publication in 1989 of the Revised English Bible to use this very readable and scholarly version as the basis of our commentaries, and we are grateful to the Oxford and Cambridge University Presses for the requisite licence. Our authors will nevertheless be free to cite and discuss other translations wherever they think that these will illuminate the original text.

Just as the books that make up the Bible differ in their provenance and purpose, so our authors will necessarily differ in the structure and bearing of their commentaries. But they will all strive to get as close as possible to the intention of the original writers, expounding their texts in the light of the place, time, circumstances, and culture that gave them birth, and showing why each work was received by Jews and Christians into their respective Canons of Holy Scripture. They will seek to make full use of the dramatic advance in biblical scholarship world-wide but at the same time to explain technical terms in the language of the common reader, and to suggest ways in which scripture can help towards the living of a Christian life today. They will endeavour to produce commentaries that can be used with confidence in ecumenical, multiracial, and multifaith situations, and not by scholars only but by preachers, teachers, students, church members, and anyone who wants to improve his or her understanding of the Bible.

Ivor H. Jones

ABBREVIATIONS

AV	Authorised Version of the Bible
GNB	Good New Bible
NEB	New English Bible
NJB	New Jerusalem Bible
NRSV	New Revised Standard Version of the Bible
REB	Revised English Bible
RV	Revised Version of the Bible

INTRODUCTION

Romans, in the Authorized Version of 1611, has wound itself into the English language: 'a law unto themselves'; 'the wages of sin is death'; 'the powers that be are ordained of God'; 'doubtful disputations'; 'the just shall live by faith'. At least those, and many more, are familiar phrases to a Protestant ear – though Catholic friends tell me that they tend to leave Romans to the Protestants and themselves make do with Ephesians. But from the Reformation onwards Romans has been one of the defining documents of Western Christianity. Can it still have comparable significance today?

The professional study of Romans is mainly directed either to discovering what Paul intended his original readers to understand or to presenting a modern form of the Reformation response to the Epistle. Those matters are what technical scholarship must properly pursue for the benefit of us all. But this commentary is a serious offering to non-technical readers who accept the Epistle's importance, are willing to follow a complex argument, but need persuading that spending thought on an ancient text from a culture vastly different from our own can help them with their needs today. It must be freely admitted that Romans does not answer modern questions, but it will be maintained that it directs attention to matters that Christians must consider and address.

It is by no means an easy letter to read. It begins and ends with greetings and information for Christian communities in Rome, but the greater part is polemical, defensive, expository, speculative, instructional, and magisterial. If we find it hard going, so must its earliest hearers. To some modern readers its contents seem so dissonant that they propose a simpler, much more coherent earlier letter, supplemented by material from a later time. Such proposals are discussed in technical commentaries where they receive little support. We shall take Romans as it is, the product of a well-stocked, energetic, and wonderfully perceptive Christian mind.

Romans as it is: a Greek text such as that put out by the Bible Societies or by Nestle-Aland of the Deutsche Bibel Stiftung. That text results from the critical study of some 5,000 Greek manuscripts containing all or parts of the New Testament, not to mention ancient translations and quotations. Experts in that field have evidence that some early copies of the Epistle ended with chapter 15, others with chapter 16. I myself have no hesitation in accepting chapters 1–16 as the original letter which was sometimes abbreviated when copied and sent elsewhere than Rome.

Even those who read it in Greek sometimes feel uncertain about Paul's line of thought and the meaning he attaches to recurrent important words. There is no remedy in attempting a literal translation – for two reasons. First, there is really no such thing: it is no more than substituting the equivalent word in a small lexicon and ignoring the characteristics of Greek syntax. Such a wooden translation sometimes produces a useful beginning and I have used it once or twice in this commentary. Secondly, Paul is the Humpty Dumpty of the New Testament. You may remember that (in *Through the Looking Glass*, chapter 6) Alice challenged his use of the word glory. 'When I use a word' he said, 'it means just what I choose it to mean – neither more nor less.' Alice replied, 'The question is whether you *can* make words mean different things,' and he replied, 'The question is, which is to be master – that's all.' Paul, who (as it were) sat on the wall that either divided Jews from Greek or marked the boundary where they could converse, also dealt masterfully with words. Modern translation is often in difficulty. What can be made of Paul's *nomos* which means usage, custom, law, when he is clearly referring to the Hebrew *torah* which means teaching. I have often used 'instruction' which can mean being told how to do and what to do. What is to be done with 'righteousness' which is now effectively meaningless? – as in a sense it always has been, since it was invented to express whatever was the meaning of the Greek noun *dikaiosyne*. When Paul has an ample stock of words to indicate wrong-doing, why does he use 'sin' as it if were a tyrannical power? Or what does he mean by 'flesh' when it is clearly neither muscular tissue nor sexual appetite?

These questions can be answered and meanings can be explained in the course of following Paul's argument. I have provided a list of important words and where their meanings are explained.

The Epworth Commentaries assume that the readers will refer to the Revised English Bible (1989). That translation has many merits including the determination to put the New Testament into vigorous modern English that reads well. In uncertain passages, where the meaning can be one thing or another, it does not equivocate but makes up its mind – in my opinion, sometimes wrongly. But every translation depends on prior understanding. The New Revised Standard Version (1989), constructed on different principles, often presents older familiar translations and is a shade nearer the wooden translation already mentioned. I would recommend it as a crib to someone learning Greek, for they would use it rather more easily to follow Paul's wording.

If readers of this commentary have the REB open at Romans, I think they will be unlikely to make frequent reference to other parts of the Bible. At times that is unavoidable because Paul often relies on statements from, say, Genesis and Isaiah, and expects them to be known and pondered. Sometimes I have copied out parts of the Old Testament in the hope that their significance will begin to appear. Sometimes I refer to the Septuagint, the translation of Hebrew Scripture into Greek, since Paul sometimes prefers it or bases an argument on it. It can be assumed that he was familiar with the more extensive Greek Old Testament (which includes the Apocrypha) since the influence of Wisdom, Ecclesiasticus, and Maccabees has been detected in Romans.

When commenting on Romans it is tempting to compare what is said here with what is said elsewhere, especially in Galatians which says much about righteousness and justification. It is tempting to build up a Pauline doctrine of salvation, for example, by supporting Romans with similar or complementary passages from elsewhere. But I have resisted such temptation, citing other Pauline letters only when what Romans says might be misunderstood without the statement from another Epistle in the primary group, namely Thessalonians, Corinthians, and Galatians written before Romans, and Philippians written after. I regard the secondary group as Colossians and Ephesians, and the tertiary group as Timothy and Titus. These could very profitably be compared with Romans, but I have not done so. All references not otherwise identified are to Romans. Quotations of a passage under discussion (in the REB translation) are printed in italics.

Where, when, and why was Romans written?

When Paul wrote chapter 16 he was in Corinth. He commends Phoebe to the Roman community, and she was 'a minister in the church at Cenchreae', the eastern port of Corinth. Paul's 'host and host of the whole congregation' was Gaius, probably the same Gaius of Corinth whom Paul had baptized (I Cor. 1.14). Paul sends greetings from him, and also from the city treasurer Erastus (16.23). According to Acts 19.22 one of Paul's assistants at Ephesus was called Erastus, and he was sent to Macedonia. According to Acts 19.21 Paul made up his mind to visit Macedonia and Achaia (northern and southern Greece) and then go on to Jerusalem. So he did and 'finally reached Greece' where he spent three months before beginning the journey to Jerusalem (Acts 20.1–3). Proceeding from the known date when Gallio was proconsul of Achaia (Acts 18.12), Paul's stay in Corinth can be placed in the middle fifties.

Paul had often wanted to visit Rome but so far without success (1.13). So what were his plans? His immediate intention was to go to Jerusalem and deliver a charitable fund collected by Christians in Macedonia and Achaia. Then he would extend his work to Spain and visit Rome on his way there (15.23–29). So the Epistle was written to engage the interest and support of the Roman community and to show them how he was thinking. But there must be more to it than that. Such an elaborate, passionately argued presentation goes far beyond a letter of introduction. What is Romans really about?

That depends on what Romans really is. Is it a treatise on the gospel, enclosed within a letter in which Paul commends himself to the Roman community? Does 'treatise' cover only 1.16–8.39, with 9–11 and 12.1–15.13 no more than useful but inessential supplements? If the treatise comprises 1.16–8.39, is it an expansion of the argument in Galatians, or a fusion of Jewish 'legal' thought from Galatians, plus Hellenistic participatory thought from Corinthians? Such a 'treatise' view is supported mainly by Western theological debate. Or, is Romans a real letter throughout, like other Pauline letters where theological argument and ethical advice are worked out in relation to the situation of the readers?

If you give thoughtful attention to 1.1–15 and 15.14–33 you will observe that Paul is vividly conscious of his apostleship to Gentiles although his main argument is based on Jewish presuppositions and is presumably addressed to Jews. The first half of the Epistle displays the conviction that the gospel is for the Jew first, and also for the Gentile. The conflict between the weak in faith and the strong (chapters 14–15), which Paul treats with close knowledge and care, leads up to an appeal that Jews and Gentiles should welcome one another in the Christian community. Paul has completed his responsibility 'from Jerusalem as far round as Illyricum' and proposes to go next to Spain. This then is a turning point in his apostolic mission. So he writes in order to involve the Roman Christians in two important enterprises: the extension of his Gentile apostleship in the West, and the preservation of the Jewish-Christian mother-community in Jerusalem, where he first must go and take the collection as a charitable gift and a symbol of the unity of Jewish and Greek communities. Finally, he must settle once for all any misunderstanding about the central importance and exact significance of the Jewish heritage within the gospel of Christ as it spreads in the Hellenistic world.

This turning point for Paul, however, was significant only because it was the indicator of a major change for the world, that is for human society as he knew it. Indeed, because it was inaugurated by the death and resurrection of the Son of God, it was the major change by which all future existence would be constituted. Paul and other early Christian writers regarded themselves as living in the last stage of 'this present world' (12.2). That is their eschatological conviction (to use a word that will not appear again in this commentary). The Greek word *eschatos* means 'last', and eschatology used to mean 'the part of theology concerned with death and final destiny' (as *The Concise Oxford Dictionary* still thinks it does). But it is now used (indeed overused) to indicate a pervasive conviction among New Testament writers that they were dealing with a world that would soon pass away and be succeeded by something new. When attempting to portray the new world they often used speculative imagery, fully aware that it was imagery and not prediction (unlike some later students of their writings who assume that end-time imagery must have been intended literally). But apart from the imagery, they identified components of the new world – as Paul points to the gift of the Spirit and the uniting of Jews and Gentiles. He is dealing with the problems of communities, not simply with the theology of individuals. Once we abandon an excessively individualistic reading of Paul's argument, we may begin to see why he thought that the change from old to new was so momentous that it had to be told in Rome, where it would have most influence.

The structure of the Epistle is indicated in the Contents listing on pp. v–vi.

Some readers of this commentary may want to know how Paul's teaching in Romans consorts with his teaching elsewhere. To them I recommend John Ziesler, *Pauline Christianity*, The Oxford Bible Series, Oxford University Press, 1990 revised edition.

Some readers may properly require fuller evidence for translations adopted and interpretations proposed. The best available one-volume commentary is by John Ziesler, *Paul's Letter to the Romans*, TPI New Testament Commentaries, SCM Press/Trinity Press International 1989. The fullest major commentary is by James D.G. Dunn, *Romans 1–8* and *Romans 9–16*, Word Biblical Commentary Vols 38A, 38B, Word Publishing 1991. This provides both comment and explanation, the comment being highly technical, the explanation somewhat simpler. Discriminating knowledge of an immense bibliography (by now of course out of date) is combined with shrewd and determined exegetical skill. The Reformed tradition of exegesis is carried on by C.K. Barrett, *The Epistle to the Romans*, Black's New Testament Commentaries, 1991 second edition; and by C.E.B. Cranfield, *A Critical and Exegetical Commentary on the Epistle to the Romans*, T. & T. Clark's International Critical Commentary Vol. I, 1975, Vol. II, 1979 (which demands knowledge of Greek and is a joy to those who possess it). Determined readers may profitably discover the demands of German scholarship in Ernst Käsemann, *Commentary on Romans*, SCM Press 1980. My own handling of some of the technical problems may be found in K. Grayston, *Dying We Live*, Darton, Longman and Todd 1990. To students of the Epistle who are able to follow the technical arguments I now commend two recent books, not that I necessarily agree with them but I find them stimulating in method and instructive in information. They are *Paul: A Critical Life* by Jerome Murphy-O'Connor, OP, Clarendon Press 1996 – a major work of imaginative historical reconstruction; and *Romans* by Robert Morgan, Sheffield Academic Press, New Testament Guides 1995, an extremely demanding account 'of the difficulties, possible interpretations, and influence of the Epistle'.

Two useful sourcebooks for students are G. Vermes, *The Dead Sea Scrolls in English*, 4th edn Penguin 1995 (for Qumran documents) and J.H. Charlesworth (ed), *The Old Testament Pseudepigapha*, 2 vols, DLT 1983, 1985 (for inter-testamental literature e.g. Pseudo-Philo).

This commentary has not been written to make Paul say what might be said if he were living now. I have tried to explain, with the necessary minimum of technical explanation, what he was saying to the people of his time – with indications here and there of how his words might stir our responses to our own different situations. I hope that readers of the commentary will be stimulated to engage with Paul's convictions as they handle the particular problems and opportunities of our time.

Over many years I have taught about the Epistle to the Romans in Bristol and elsewhere – including a most agreeable term in the University of Glasgow. I have profited from the responses of students and colleagues. Most recently I owe a very great debt to my friend and colleague, the Revd John D. Clapham who has commented fully on the draft script, prompting reconsiderations and saving me from many blunders. Errors that remain are mine.

What Paul said about the Spirit and how it could be expressed was the subject of conversation on the last walk I had with my wife. The doctrine of death and resurrection that gives me comfort is slowly turning into Pauline hope.

Paul introduces himself and his reasons for visiting Rome
1.1–15

1.1 He presents himself (by using *servant*, or slave) in a way we find objectionable – as did the ancient Greeks, though not the Jews. *Servant* and master (or lord) form a word-pair: a lord was a master who both gave orders to his servants and, if sensible, protected them as his household and responsibility. Paul is therefore acting under instructions laid down and demonstrated by Jesus Christ our Lord (v. 4) and in this respect, is like all Christians. So he is in being *called by God*. The thought of calling plays a well-known role in Paul: it describes God's approach to the human race, calling us into being (4.17), inviting us to receive his grace and to grasp his freedom, presenting us with an identity and function as his sacred people (v. 7) and making some his agents: *called by God* to be an apostle.

In that respect Paul is marked out from the readers of his letter. The word *apostle* (meaning 'someone sent') had no interesting usage in the Greek world, though there was something similar in Jewish life for an authorized representative. Here Paul is an agent of the gospel *to bring people of all nations to faith and obedience* (v. 5; 11.13). For this task he is set apart from his own passionate Pharisaic allegiance (as he says in Phil. 3.4–7) to serve the revised divine intention. Formerly God had demanded a clear separation between Israel and the heathen (Lev. 20.26: 'You must be holy to me, because I the Lord am holy. I have made a clear separation between you and the heathen, that you may belong to me'). But now in Christ Jesus he was drawing Jews and the heathen together. This in part is the good news about God, especially as he does it out of love, conferring both grace and peace (v. 7).

1.2 This way of regarding God is not novel: it was *announced beforehand in sacred scriptures through his prophets*, though according to 16.25–26 it was a 'divine secret kept in silence for long ages but now disclosed, and … made known to all nations through prophetic scriptures'. It looks as if modern readers will make little of Paul's

1

argument unless they give some thought to the prophets. In fact Paul often quotes scripture, introduced by 'as it is written', or similar phrases, drawing more or less equally on three of the four main divisions of the Hebrew Bible, namely the Instruction (Genesis to Deuteronomy), the later Prophets (mostly Isaiah), and the Writings (mostly Psalms). At significant points in Isaiah the announcement of good news is made: 'You that bring good news to Zion; raise your voice …' (Isa. 40.9–11); 'How beautiful on the mountains are the feet of the herald, the bringer of good news' … (Isa. 52.7–10, quoted in Rom. 10.15); and 'The Lord … has sent me to announce good news to the humble … to proclaim a year of the Lord's favour and a day of the vengeance of our God …' (Isa. 61.1–3). This, however, is for the benefit of Zion i.e. the Jewish community: but in Paul's understanding of the gospel it is too slight a task for his servant to being back the survivors of Israel. God therefore appoints him as a light to the nations so that his salvation may reach to earth's farthest bounds (Isa. 49.6). Hence the Epistle raises the questions: who are the people that receive God's love, and on what conditions?

1.3–4   The gospel refers to God's activity in 'raising the dead' which is symbolic language for the transformation of whole communities (as in the famous imagery of Ezek. 37) by God's destruction of their former life and his replacement of it by a new unexpected life. In this preliminary statement of the gospel it is resurrection that has emphasis, and it is the resurrection of God's *son*. Every Jew would remember that 'Israel is my firstborn son' (Ex. 4.22) and that one man, a descendant of David, could represent the people of God under his promise that 'I shall be a father to him, and he will be my son' (II Sam. 7.14). Jesus Christ indeed represents the people of God, descended from David, in all its frailty (which is what *on the human level* really implies); but he was established (rather than *proclaimed*) Son of God in *power* when he was *raised from the dead* by *the Spirit* (see 8.11) that consecrates those who are *called to be* God's *people* (v. 7).

1.5–6   Paul's *apostolic commission* was to act in the *name* of Jesus Christ and promote *faith and obedience* among *people of all nations*. Since this theme is repeated at the end of the letter (16.19, 26) it may be treated as an acceptable summary of Paul's main intention. But what does it mean? Is it *faith* in God or Christ, and *obedience* to the Mosaic commandments or, come to that, any other commandments? It depends on the meaning of *obedience*. In common use it means 'doing what we're told to do', but in the Bible it means a favourable or dutiful response. Here it implies a favourable response to God's act in raising Christ from the dead, and making reliance (*faith*) on that act the foundation of a plural Christian community in Rome. Paul regards his *commission* as a *privilege*, i.e. it is a mark of God's grace, which is his noble generosity to people who are certainly undeserving and may also be resentful.

1.7   Hence the community in Rome, which may not be unfamiliar with hostility against God, is offered the double benefit of experiencing his generosity and being at peace with him. *God is our father*, the source, provider and protector of our life; *Jesus Christ* is our *lord*, that is our life's director and protector.

1.8–15   Paul now begins to explain the purpose of his letter: it is a necessary introduction to his proposed visit (a plan developed in 15.14–33). As an apostle he is of course responsible to God *to whom I offer the service of my spirit by preaching the gospel of his Son*, so he begins by thanking him (contrast the irreligious attitude described in 1.21). Paul's gratitude is not for status but for his work-load, which gives him a responsibility even to Christians who were not his own converts. Their faith was not private but known publicly (the meaning of *all over the world*) and took diverse forms (hence the reference to *all of you in Rome*). There were Jews and Gentiles (see 1.16), and Paul has a special responsibility *to Greek and non-Greek, to learned and simple*. So far he has done his best by continually praying for them – not, one suspects, by putting them in an intercessions list, but by discovering their needs (such as turn up in chapters 12–15) and working out with the Divine Wisdom how they could be met. But now the Roman community stands on the way of his proposed journey to Spain, either to help or hinder. So in rather embarrassed language, he hints that Rome might be included within his responsibility for *the gentile world*, that he might strengthen them with *some spiritual gift* – or better still, that he and they might *be encouraged by one another's faith*. Yet it was right for an apostle, even when addressing a church of such widely reputed faith, to tell them that strength is maintained, perhaps improved, by considering what the gospel is and preaching it.

What the gospel is
1.16–17

Why then does he say *I am not ashamed of the gospel*? By the *gospel* he means the saving consequences of the death and resurrection of Jesus who was and is God's anointed (Christ i.e. specially appointed) son and agent. That Jesus died by the shameful death of crucifixion is the essence of the matter (it had to remain scandalous), and Paul so preached it from the beginning, as he insists in I Cor. 1.23–24. Something else must have been said to prompt Paul's defensive assertion.

Today, of course, the gospel (or what people take to be the gospel) is widely regarded as shameful, sometimes by Christians as well as non-Christians. It requires, they say, an absurd mythology of the supernatural, or its explanation why God required Jesus to die is unbelievable, or its insistence on forgiveness condones wrong-doing, or it imposes a restricted Judaeo-Christian morality. And often Paul is the whipping-boy for all that seems shameful in the gospel. Often when Christians today hear what purports to be the gospel they too cannot easily push shame aside.

Whether Paul's lack of shame can help us remains to be seen. What he asserted must have arisen as a reply to criticism – that his way of presenting the gospel was shameful because he offered it to Gentiles without first enrolling them in God's (Jewish) people, and on the condition of faith without demanding obedience to the Mosaic Instruction (usually called 'law'). Thus 'his' gospel is anti-Jewish and indifferent to morality. In chapters 9–11 which give careful thought to the future of the Jews, Paul twice quotes Isa. 28.16: 'Here I lay in Zion a stone to trip over, a rock to stumble against; but he who has faith in it will not be put to shame', explicitly referring to acceptance by faith, not law (9.30–33) and for both Jew and Greek (10.11–12).

Paul begins his answer to these charges (which will take up the rest of the letter) by a thematic statement i.e. a sentence that presents the essential convictions – the power of God, salvation, Jews and Greeks, righteousness, faith, and life – from which all else can be developed when brought to an awareness of Jesus Christ. The *power of God*, already demonstrated in the resurrection of the Son of God (1.4), is available in the gospel for the people of God – *the Jew first* certainly, *but the Greek also*. Paul is convinced that 'the same Lord is Lord of all' so that (in respect of faith, at least) 'there is no distinction between Jew and Greek' (10.12). In other matters, Greek thought had influenced Jewish life and Jewish devotion had prompted Greek interest. When presenting the gospel, Paul could not ignore this inter-penetration of two diverse cultures – both of which needed God's *saving power*. The words 'save' and 'salvation' can be used very widely to indicate deliverance from peril and restoration to wholeness but Paul used them only in relation to God. Hence they have become religious words and, under the influence of Western individualism, salvation can mean our 'eventual safe passage through human trials and divine judgment to eternal bliss'. But more properly salvation is a social need and happening. Paul is here concerned less with individual piety, more with the moral and religious fate of social groups, Jews and Greeks – with a significant priority given to the Jews, whose salvation is specially considered in chapters 9–11. But social salvation – the rescue of a community from its degradation and the disclosure of hitherto unseen possibilities – is available only if each and every member exercises *faith*. What Paul intends by that word will appear in the course of the letter – certainly trust in God's power and his nearness to help – but it is useful to consider what the word means in modern English. According to the *Concise Oxford Dictionary*, *faith* means 'complete trust or confidence', and then 'firm belief, especially without logical proof' (or, it would be sensible to add, 'without satisfactory evidence'). 'Trust' and 'confidence' are excellent descriptions of faith; but Paul's firm belief (which can be presented with sensible persuasion) is much more a new perception of the human situation. In effect Paul says 'When I was a persecuting Pharisee, I thought that the desperate human situation could be dealt with by blameless practice of every part of the Jewish law (as he would later tell the Philippians, 3.5–6). But now I have encountered what God has done in the death and resurrection of his Son, I have a very different understanding of the desperate human situation.' This had come to him as a revelation of the *righteousness of God*, which the Jerusalem Bible translates as 'the saving justice of God'. This properly suggests that we are concerned with what is right and just in a community; but 'righteousness' has long been a word without resonance in modern English; and 'justice' too readily calls up thoughts of a remote, perplexing, and expensive legal system. But God is not our Judge, he is our Father (as Paul has already said in verse 7, and will say again at 8.15). He is the head of

5

the household, providing what they need to live, protecting them in danger, restraining and punishing them when they do wrong. Now that is precisely what Paul (speaking from Jewish covenant experience) would intend by the *righteousness of God*. God does what is right for his people, saving them not only from hostility but also from their own stupid and wicked actions. In that sense it is his saving goodness *seen at work, beginning in faith and ending in faith* – meaning perhaps that it begins with the utter fidelity of God and leads to the Christian life of faith, or perhaps inviting us to explore the full extent of trust and confidence in our dealings with God.

Paul now quotes *scripture* to show that his new perception is not an unsupported novelty but can be discovered (by the alert reader) in the sacred writings of Israel's past. Like his contemporaries, he does not rest content with the first thought that comes to mind but lets his imagination play round with possible implications. He turns to the prophet Habakkuk (as did the writers of the Dead Sea Scrolls) who was instructed by the Lord to write down, in the most readable way, a vision for the appointed time – with this assurance, that 'The reckless will lack an assured future, while the righteous will live by being faithful' (Hab.2.4). But to what or whom? The Scrolls Sect said 'faithful to their founder, the Teacher of Righteousness', so Paul could have said 'to Jesus Christ'. When Habakkuk was put into Greek, the righteous lived by God's fidelity; and Paul could well have said that. Recently a different way of reading his words has become popular, as in REB: *Whoever is justified by faith shall gain life*. That may better suit Paul's argument and the plan of his letter, but it introduces the tiresome verb 'justify' before it is necessary. NJB has 'upright by faith' to avoid 'righteous' which has now no currency in normal English. A 'righteous' person is one who 'behaves acceptably in his community'; so we could translate Paul's quotation thus: Anyone who behaves acceptably lives by his complete confidence (in God).

So much for Paul's careful introduction and his sharp hint that the gospel will be defended. If he has to answer the suspicion that he is easy-going about morality and indifferent to the Jewish people, then let his old Pharisaic voice be raised. In 1.18–32 an unmeasured attack is made on Greek religion and morals – leading (Paul supposes) to gratified approval from some of his hearers. So, whether they be Jew or Greek, in 2.1–16 he turns his criticism upon them – because, in his understanding of the good news, God will finally expose and judge the things we human beings try to keep secret from ourselves. With a solitary reference to Jesus Christ (v. 16), Paul is now ready, in 2.17–29 to turn a Pharisaic passion for moral purity against his own Jewish people.

Wickedness among Gentiles and Jews
1.18–3.20

1.18 *Divine retribution* replaces the familiar words 'wrath of God'; and 'wrath' (which is now a comic word, like a mother-in-law joke) gives way in ten other places to *retribution* which is a very literary word and nowadays means requital for wickedness. The basic meaning of Paul's word is anger and its unpleasant consequences. In the ancient world severe, unexpected, and inexplicable events were commonly ascribed to the anger of the gods, and the Old Testament has numerous examples (e.g. Job 14; Ps. 90.7–12). Such ruthlessness injured the reputation of the gods: their anger produced no permanent improvement in human behaviour, so that the gods appeared both savage and stupid. This archaic imagery began to be obsolete in 1660 when the announcement of Boyle's Law marked the real beginning of experimental science. In our own day, we find ourselves in a world still undergoing major structural changes, where whatever happens can be understood by discovered principles (or will be), and where our existence is determined by the course of nature, by our own interventions, and by sheer chance. In that complex situation we need from God not angry threats but indications of what to do and what help is at hand, together with the solid conviction that in every situation he is unalterably opposed to what is cruel and destructive. God's displeasure has something of the right meaning, but too easily suggests remote indignation. 'Anger' indicates readiness to act, and the old word should be kept until we have seen what Paul makes of this ancient metaphor.

1.19–23 It is Paul's basic conviction that heaven and earth, and all forms of existence are governed by wisdom and knowledge (see 11.33–36). Hence *impiety* is disrespect for the divine wisdom, and *wickedness* is deliberate flouting of wisdom in social life. Therefore what is wrong with *impiety and wickedness* is not that they offend God but that they *suppress the truth* about human existence. And that is what the Greeks are said to do. It is not denied that they have some awareness of God: *indeed God himself has disclosed it to them.* Using the kind of argument set out in the Wisdom of Solomon 13–14, Paul indicates that Greek intelligence could move from the seen to the unseen. Since the world is questionably eternal, self-maintaining, or permanent there may well be *unseen* sources of its existence: *everlasting power and deity*, meaning unlimited energy and constructive use of it. Even with such a limited way of *knowing God*, the Greeks who rightly *boast of their wisdom* and *all their thinking* should have decided *to honour him as God, and to render him thanks*. But they did not. *They ended in futility* and *made fools of themselves. Their conduct is indefensible.*

So it seemed to the passionate Pharisee. But how can you give thanks and honour to a source of unlimited energy? Especially when ordinary life for most people was precarious, sordid, and unfair? Few literate Jews tried to understand why pagan religion used *an image shaped like a mortal man, even images like birds, beasts, and reptiles*. A human cult hero had achieved success: perhaps his model might help less fortunate people. Many birds, beasts, and reptiles responded more adequately to stress than human families: perhaps their virtues might be acquired. And many Jews in the course of Israel's history thought so too. But the central conviction of Jewish religion is attached to a God who through his agents speaks, who does not have to be deduced from observation of *the things that he has made*, who discloses himself and imparts his glory to those who accept the world with gratitude. In Judaism faith is thankful acceptance of what God offers; idolatry is the attempt to screw reluctant benefits out of whatever gods there be.

In our own day there is major disbelief in a God to be honoured and thanked, even among Christians – probably because the church's teachers have failed to make a sensible case for such a faith. The cruder forms of idolatry are reviving, role models are commercially exploited, and games of chance and lotteries are major parts of everyday life. Not that everyone is taken in, but we inhabit a social culture that encourages idolatry and suppresses the truth about human existence.

1.24   With what consequences? Three times Paul says *God has given them up* (vv. 24, 26, 28) – not, as it were, disclaiming responsibility but handing them over to the consequences of what they had persistently chosen to do. God is occupied, not (as many suppose) in devising and applying punishments for misdemeanours, but in rescuing us from the unpleasantness of misbehaving. One of the problems about God is not his severity but his forbearance (3.25). *Divine retribution*, his anger against wickedness, takes the form of allowing the dreadful consequences of wrong-doing to operate so that we know we are self-punished. Even if Paul is not yet speaking with a fully Christian voice, what he says at this point puts a question against the fairly widespread assumption that Christians must promptly forgive any kind of wrongdoing. Although forgiveness is an important biblical theme (for example, 4.7 quoting Ps. 32), Paul does not use the standard word for 'forgiveness' in Romans or any of his primary letters.

1.25   The denunciation of Gentile morals is rhetorical and partly conventional. But neither rhetoric nor convention is to be despised. Rhetoric may sometimes be a passionate affirmation of the truth, and convention may often convey the necessary conditions of social stability. Paul was not saying that every Gentile was a thoroughly wicked person (see 2.14–15) but that all Gentiles lived in a society that made wickedness possible, and encouraged it. In such a society people exchanged *the truth of God for a lie* (the God-given truth about human existence replaced by what was known to be untrue). They *offered reverence and worship to created things*, as if power and splendour resided in them (consider what is said about the frustration, mortality, and anguish of creation in 8.20–22) *instead of to the Creator*. We use and enjoy the creation only if we accept it thankfully from God and say *Blessed is he for ever*. But the Gentiles *have not seen fit to acknowledge God* even though *they know well enough the just decree of God that those who behave* as they do *deserve to die* – where the stress falls on 'deserve' i.e. such activities are recognizably life-destroying.

1.26–27   What then are the dreadful activities? Here REB produces an indignant splutter, rather than a useful translation. Paul says (v. 24) that *God has given them up*, in their self-willed determination, to uncleanness. This 'determination' is suggested by a word that appears again later, sometimes as 'coveting', an obsession with acquiring and appropriating. Paul's contemporary, the Jewish philosopher Philo, defined it as 'pulling and dragging someone in spite of himself towards what he has not got'. Under that compulsion people are given up to uncleanness: they contaminate whatever they touch. Ideas of clean and unclean are puzzlingly complex, but in the biblical world what is unclean is often dangerous. We know the risks of uncleanness in a hospital theatre, in a swimming pool, in a restaurant kitchen, and so on. Uncleanness is not simply disgusting, but high-risk contamination and ruin.

Such ruinous behaviour may be present in sexual intercourse and in social intercourse. *The consequent degradation of their bodies* points to erotic genital activity by females with females and by males with males. Here Paul was expressing a consistent, deeply-rooted Jewish repulsion against homosexual genital activity, regarded as unnatural and forbidden, and producing its own unpleasant consequences. Philo points to the unnatural confusion of the active and passive roles in sexual union, to the consequent likelihood of sterile semen, and the affliction of a female disease (*On Abraham*, 135–137). That mixture of male prejudice and popular rumour suggests that Philo did not express the enormity of the problem; nor perhaps did Paul. Erotic activity of a kind that is repulsive to many can take place between men and women or can flourish in the sexual abuse of children. Such actions are wrong, not because they are unnatural or prohibited by scripture, but because they may be a forced violation of sexual privacy, may lead to mortal danger, and in our time are destabilizing, even ruining, whole communities. No biblical commandment prohibits love between men and men, between women and women; nor does it prohibit appropriate sexual expressions of love – unless those expressions are destructive of love and community. Paul did well to put this matter on the Christian agenda; but we must deal with it in the light of our own knowledge, understanding, and experience.

1.28–31   As far as the social scene is concerned, God has given the Gentiles up to *their own depraved way of thinking, and this leads them to break all rules of conduct*. That heavy NEB translation suggests that Paul was speaking with passion though not thought. But not so; something more like this: God gave them up to a mind unfit to judge what is sensible and responsible in a social group – so that everyday life becomes riddled with nastiness. Paul makes the point with a list of vices (common in ancient moral teaching) which is more than a standard tirade. Since wrong-doing takes many forms, his words can be translated in many ways. The following may be somewhat near his intention. The debased life of a society that knows but ignores God is filled with unfairness, wickedness, ruthless self-assertion, and malice. People manipulating the resources of society are a mass of envy, murder, wrangling, treachery, and spite. They spread slander in secret and in the open, they are hostile to God, rude, arrogant, boastful, inventing new kinds of vice, without respect for parents. They lack sense, loyalty, affection, and pity. *They not only do these things themselves but approve such conduct in others*. They undermine social pressure against wrong-doing.

An unsympathetic reader might dismiss that as the predictable outpouring of a traditionally religious person in a period of rapid social change. An even more unsympathetic reader might well say that people who acknowledge God act just as badly – perhaps because secretly they hate God – and Christians would have to admit the charge. Paul's list of vices is a discouraging portrait, perhaps of his world, certainly of ours. Sharp awareness of these destructive forces gives point to Paul's cautious approval (in chapter 13) of 'the authorities in power'.

2.1–6 But at this point in the reading of the letter, Paul imagines sober approval of his attack – as it were: 'Well said. We've often passed the same judgments, and have called on God to punish these people. We can't understand why he puts up with this Gentile immorality.' From just such a person, perhaps, Paul had heard the criticism that he failed to insist on Gentile converts performing the Mosaic law. So he sets up a thorough but surprising demand for performance. (Though this is not evident in REB, there are 'per-formance' words in verses 1, 2, 3, 6, 7, 9, 10, 13, 14, and 15.) The argument goes something like this:

If you *sit in judgment* against an offender
[and do nothing more]
you condemn yourself as equally guilty;
for in passing judgment and doing no more
you commit the same offence
[because you too do not obey God's instructions].

The Pharisee knew that to condemn, disapprove, and do nothing was to be guilty before God. Hence Paul's self-description: 'In my practise of the law a Pharisee, in zeal for religion a persecutor of the church' (Phil. 3.5–6). The trouble, of course, is that over large areas of common life zeal, protests, defiance can do very little to remove our culpable participation in social wrongdoing. If for example, in our own day, we disapprove of the export of arms (subsidized by our taxes) to dubious regimes, we must realize that the UK arms industry keeps 400,000 people at work. Or if we are alarmed by atmospheric pollution, but being elderly and poorly mobile, can move only by using a car to visit shops and surgery, we join the polluters. In the 1930s Reinhold Niebuhr invented the (now politi-cally incorrect) title *Moral Man and Immoral Society*, which exactly present the dilemma. *God's judgment* operates according to the truth of the human situation, not (as REB says) *is just*. How can it be just or fair, we might say, to condemn us who detest wrong-doing but are helplessly caught up in social wrongs? We are partly responsible, perhaps, but are not to blame. But God judges things as they are – *do you imagine that you, any more than they, will escape the judgment of God?* Indeed, when we allow ourselves to realize the dreadful conditions in which mankind has long lived, and will go on living, is it not possible that God's judgment is the one hope that can save us from total despair? Why then is it so long in taking full effect? *Do you despise his wealth of kindness and tolerance and patience, failing to see that God's kindness is meant to lead you to repentance?*

In English *repentance* means regret for mistakes or wrongdoing, but Paul's word means much more: a major change of attitude and practice, an about-turn. The next sentence speaks of *obstinate impenitence*, a sturdy refusal to shift one centimetre from a fixed course of action. In II Cor. 7.9–10 'repentance' is 'a change of heart leading to salvation' (similarly in II Tim.2.25). Apart from that, Paul does not use the word – which is surprising since Jewish social life was regularly maintained by admission of wrong-doing, expression of regret, restitution (if necessary and possible), and a fine in the form of a sacrifice. That effective procedure applied to mistakes, accidents, carelessness, and sudden temptations – but not to deliberate defiance of God or to inbuilt hostility to him. And with that latter situation Paul was particularly concerned, *for the impenitent heart is laying up a store of retribution* (anger against sin) *against the day of retribution, when God's just judgment will be revealed, and he will pay everyone for what he has done.*

2.7–11   That is a conviction of faith, for it is not obviously true – for 'the wicked prosper …, they are not in trouble like ordinary mortals …; they wear pride like a necklace and violence like a robe that wraps them round …; their slanders reach up to heaven …; they say 'Does the Most High know or care?' (Ps. 73.1–12). To which question Paul's answer would be: Yes, he knows and cares, but not like a judge handing down a belated verdict and punishment; more like a father (or an old-fashioned Bantu tribal chief) trying to make it possible for the family (or the tribe) to stay together and live together. Actions have consequences; wicked actions have bad consequences. In the kindness, tolerance, and patience of his rule he shields us from the worst damage. But in the end, if we firmly reject his forbearance, he hands us over to the consequences of our actions. Rewards and punishments are not arbitrary but derive from what we have done. On one side are those who have *steady persistence in well-doing* (note that Pharisaic insistence), who pursue *glory and honour* (what God intended for mankind according to Ps. 8.5; *glory* is a key-word in Romans for proper human existence) *and immortality* (a life beyond the ravages of worldly experience): to them *God will give eternal life. For everyone who does right there will be glory, honour, and peace* (a life transformed by the removal of hostility towards God). On the other side, *those governed by selfish ambition, who refuse obedience to* the *truth* (of human existence, as God intended it) *and take evil for their guide* will experience *the retribution of his wrath*, namely *affliction and distress*.

To many readers of this passage, both the simple and the learned, verse 6 seems to deny the main conviction of Romans, namely that everyone is saved by faith, not by *what he has done*. That impression arises from the judgment language which perhaps implies a legal verdict. But according to *The Concise Oxford Dictionary* in modern English, judgment first means discernment, good sense, an opinion or estimate – and only then the sentence of a judge. So indeed it is with Paul: in verses 1 and 3 it is the readers of his Epistle who make judgments, though REB gives it a legal impression by *sit in judgment* in verse 1, and by *crimes* in verses 2 and 3 (not present in Greek). But if God is the supreme Judge, what business has he in verse 4 with *kindness and tolerance and patience*? Yet if he is Father he has every right. A proper father treats all his children entirely as a matter of grace – as best he can caring for them, protecting them, preparing them for their next responsibility in the family structure, keeping them always in mind. And since each child is in some way different, he judges them – sums them up, sees where they most need rebuke or encouragement, warning or opportunity, on the basis of what they do. If his children show *obstinate impenitence* towards his guidance, he withdraws his aid and allows *those who are governed by selfish ambition, who refuse obedience to* the *truth and take evil for their guide* to take the unpleasant consequences of their actions.

We understand Paul when he says that the benefits are *for the Jew first – and also for the Greek*; and might expect him to add that the punishments are for the Greeks first – and also for Jews. But in fact he repeats what he first said: *for the Jew first and for the Greek also –* and adds: *God has no favourites*. That conviction was well-known in Judaism – precisely because in the ancient world opponents in a dispute might hope to win by favouritism and bribery. Deuteronomy 10.17 says that God 'is no respecter of persons; he is not to be bribed; he secures justice for the fatherless and the widow, and he shows love towards the alien who lives among you'. That may well have had a pointed application to Jewish members of the church at Rome as they responded to Gentile Christians. Paul's conviction that he was commissioned to bring people of all nations to faith (1.5) goes further, and it could not have been easily acceptable to those who treasured God's promise that 'you are a people holy to the Lord your

God, and he has chosen you out of all peoples on earth to be his special possession' (Deut. 14.2). But Paul had made the necessary shift in perception. So, according to Acts 10.34, had Peter, who says Father 'to him who judges everyone impartially on the basis of what they have done' (I Peter 1.17). In the course of history such shifts become possible, even necessary; and if they happen, one epoch comes to an end (not without a struggle) and a new epoch begins. In our own days, we have to decide whether to stand alongside a God who has no favourites – as regards women and men, different kinds of family, black people and white people, orientals and Westerners.

A little earlier it was said that 'in the end God hands us over to the consequences of our actions', pointing forward to *the day of retribution* when there is no longer a shield against the results of wrong-doing. There is a strong sense that this present age is on the way to its end, and readers are urged not to follow its pattern (12.2). Nowhere does Paul talk of a new age, but much is said about the remarkable possibilities opened up by the resurrection of Christ and briefly introduced in verse 7 as *eternal life*. That indeed is the opposite of death (as is plain in 5.21 and 6.23) and it has that quality because it shares in the life of the Eternal Being. But there is no encouragement to imagine a literal Great Assize followed by the end of earthly existence. The vivid verbal imagery of the ancient Near East loses its force if prosaically taken over by the visual literalism familiar to the Western world. In the long history of Europe, more than once people have felt, and rightly felt, that their world was coming to an end. Basic conditions changed, new expectations were possible, different responses were required. In the last twenty years of our era, our own world has been radically changed by the new information technology and genetic engineering. Paul's words may guide us in dealing with our own 'end time', and make us ask what bearing Christ has upon it.

2.12–13   Returning to Paul's argument: is it really possible to offer Jews and Greeks an equal-opportunities policy? Surely the Jews possess an advantage denied to the Greeks, namely God's law delivered to them by Moses! The rather brusque reply is to this effect: those who have sinned where the law is not known will come to a bad end without the protection of the law; and those who have sinned where the law is known will be condemned by the law. *None will be* acceptable to *God by hearing the law, but by doing it*. REB has *None will be justified before God*. When 1.17 was under discussion, 'justify' was called a tiresome verb, chiefly because it is specially important in Romans and Galatians. It had a range of meanings in

Greek civic life and a rather different range in Jewish religious life, and was translated into English by the Latin verb 'justify' though the related adjective used the Germanic 'right'. The best way to understand it is to remember such a sentence as 'In the circumstances, we thought what he did was justified' – meaning that it was appropriate and acceptable. Thus God judges our behaviour acceptable not because we possess his law, hear it spoken, commit it to memory, discuss it, reverence it, and find it enchanting – all that we must do – but because we allow it to become the living word of God in our situation – and perform it. So it will be (moving straight from v. 13 to v. 16) *on the day when, according to my gospel, God will judge the secrets of human hearts through Christ Jesus.*

2.16   A day of judgment is important to the gospel. Dreadful things cannot go on for ever despite God's disapproval; and it must now and again be possible to say, for example, that the death penalty for theft has had its day. On this day, however, that Paul speaks of, a final decision is made about our *secrets* that God knows so well (as Jewish piety acknowledges – see Ps. 139), ambitions and motives that we conceal from other people, even from ourselves. As Paul says later, 'Each of us will be answerable to God' (14.12). And *God will judge through Jesus Christ* – a thought already conveyed to the Christians of Corinth (I Cor. 4.5 and II Cor. 5.10) and, according to Luke, preached by both Peter and Paul (Acts 10.42 and 17.31). The familiar imagery of the enthroned Son of Man separating sheep from goats (Matt. 25.31–46) is less significant than the tests of behaviour on which judgments are made; and in any case should be put alongside 'Who set me over you to judge or arbitrate?' (Luke 12.14). In the Fourth Gospel 'the Father does not judge anyone, but has given full jurisdiction to the Son' (John 5.22, 27) and, as we read his story, we discover what happens to him as judge – namely death and resurrection. In Romans, as we shall see, we who are to be judged, share death and resurrection with Christ Jesus.

2.14–15   One more thing must be said about Gentiles, because some of them, though lacking Mosaic law, do what it required. By behaving (as it seems to them) naturally, their actual social existence is law for themselves. Not what we mean by 'a law unto themselves' (i.e. they can make their own laws and do as they please) but an inner awareness of what is required by civil life, by the promptings of a bad conscience when things go wrong, and *their own thoughts argue the case, sometimes against them, sometimes even for them.* Does it not almost look as if Gentiles have *what the law requires inscribed on their hearts* which was the very thing promised in Jeremiah's new covenant: 'I shall set my law within them, writing it on their hearts.' Not, however, the continuation of that promise: 'I shall be their God, and they will be my people. No longer need they teach one another, neighbour or brother, to know the Lord; all of them, high and low alike, will know me, says the Lord, for I shall forgive their wrong-doing, and their sin I shall call to mind no more' (Jer. 31.33–34).

When you take non-religious morality deriving from civil experience and needs, backed by conscience, open to debate and not hampered by oppressive legislation, and put it against religious morality from remote tradition, backed by religious threats, presented as unquestionable, and sometimes fanatically enforced, the choice at first sight seems not in doubt. It is indeed true that religious morality must respond to developments in civil experience, accept restraints of conscience (a distinctively Greek idea), be open to debate, and abandon compulsion. But it must also be recognized that civil experience may reflect only the holders of power, that conscience must be trained and can be perverted, that discussion can be denied to a depressed class (like the slaves in ancient society), and that non-religious societies usually develop bastard forms of religion. They need a Lord for high and low who can forgive their wrong-doing.

2.17–20   Paul now turns to the justifiable claims of Jewish life and religion, distinguished from Gentile life by reliance on the Instruction (law). Addressing an imagined Jewish companion, he says *You take pride in your God*. He feels elation and satisfaction in the Divine Being, so different from the solemn reserve of many Western Christians. Paul is using a favourite word (often translated by boast, exult, rejoice), sometimes with approval (exulting in God, 5.11; in the Instruction, 2.23; in the hope of the divine glory, 5.2; in hardships, 5.3; in the service of God, 15.17); sometimes with disapproval, when it implies self-satisfaction (3.27; 4.2) or contempt for Jews (11.18). A Jew knows the divine will; from the Instruction he discriminates between what is meaningful and what is not. He is *a guide to the blind* and *a light to those in darkness* (as in Isa. 42.6–7; 49.6 – Wisd. 18.4 speaks of 'your people, through whom the imperishable light of the law was to be given to the world'), an instructor of the foolish, and a teacher of the immature (as Wisdom claims to be in Prov. 1.20–23) because *in the law* he possesses *the embodiment of knowledge and truth*. What a fine commendation of Pharisaic religion which gives meaningful instructions, conveys illumination that can be taught even to foolish and immature people!

2.21–23 But knowledge and truth must be embodied not in written or remembered words but in people's actions. If a Jew is *a thief*, or *an adulterer*, or commits sacrilege (it is not known what kind of religious violation is meant) he dishonours God by *breaking the law* – which reads like an adaptation of Isa. 52.5, where the Lord is despised by Gentiles for allowing the oppression of his people; but now the Lord is despised for the bad behaviour of his people. This is scarcely a wholesale condemnation of all Jews, or even of Jews as a community. It is an argument addressed to a single Jew, and the charges are conventional – for instance, Paul's contemporary Philo mentions theft, adultery, murder, and sacrilege. The thrust of the argument is this: if you are confident in your possession of the law, can you be equally confident of your performance of the law, you and your fellow Jews? What damage can you do to God, to Jewish people, and to the law itself! A reflection that Christians can readily apply to themselves.

2.24–29 When Paul set out his Jewish credentials, he included 'circumcised on my eighth day … a Hebrew born and bred' (Phil. 3.5). That was an essential requirement of every male child for membership of the covenant people (Gen. 17.10–14 and elsewhere) though not a sufficient requirement. Circumcision was widely practised in the ancient world (as it is today) and so did not distinguish Jews from (say) Arabs. Hence the insistence that the external sign should point to a corresponding inner devotion: 'circumcise yourselves to the service of the Lord, circumcise your hearts' (Jer. 4.4; Deut. 10.16; 30.6). But the Hellenistic world regarded circumcision as indecorous and perverse. No Jew could forget the Maccabaean revolt (some one hundred and eighty years before the time when Paul was writing), bitterly fought against the Syrian emperor's attack on Jewish identity by prohibiting circumcision. In Paul's day some Jewish Christians tried to insist that converts from Gentile religion should be circumcised: 'Those Gentiles must be circumcised and told to keep the law of Moses' (Acts 15.5). The Jerusalem apostles, and Paul in his Galatian letter, said No. But here he goes further.

It is easy enough to follow Paul's argument in a superficial way. If circumcision conveys the greatest of benefits, then there are rules that go with the benefits; and refusal to obey the rules cancels the circumcision. Correspondingly, if an uncircumcised man obeys the rules, could it not be deemed that he was circumcised? Every civil servant and academic knows that device for dealing with specially deserving cases. But that assumes the formal, not the essential importance of circumcision. It is difficult for a Western Christian to capture the sensitivity of a first-century Jew of the Levant. But we are all familiar with the practice – perhaps involved in it – of stressing, altering, adorning, marring, or removing some bodily feature to signal our kind of personal or communal statement. Hair is the commonest example. Now circumcision is a most intimate signal of that sort, normally concealed but daily obvious to a male person who can say 'This sign, given by my religion and my parents, makes me a Jew with his high privileges, responsibilities, and dangers.' But for Paul this was one of the things he counted as sheer loss for the sake of knowing Jesus Christ his Lord (Phil. 3.8).

No one would have seriously disputed Paul's insistence that a Jew who disobeyed the Instruction was debasing his circumcision. A Jew is not to be identified by external marks (after all, Arabs too are Semites and circumcised) but by an inward determination that is open to spiritual power and not limited by written commands. (The ancient world treated writing with great respect but with caution: a written command both limited what could be done and prompted devices for evasion.) Only God can command that inward determination – even if (especially if) it was present in Gentiles. *He may be physically uncircumcised, but by fulfilling the law he will pass judgment on you who break it, for all your written code and circumcision.* Paul has thus taken the great leap in perception: he no longer says that circumcision must be inward as well as outward, but that inward circumcision replaces outward. Or, to put it differently, Jewish circumcision is no longer a mark of Jewish separation from the rest of humanity but an indicator of their service for God in rescuing mankind as a whole (as will appear plainly in 15.8–12)

Christian readers today ought to know that modern Jewish authorities are hostile to Paul for taking up this position. Christians who are persuaded by Paul ought at least to examine their own symbols of identity and consider whether they promote or hinder God's universal goodness.

3.1–6   Paul does not, however, deprive Jews and circumcision of *advantage*, which is *great, in every way* – lovingly named in 9.4–5 when he turns his thoughts to the rescue of his kinsfolk. But here, with an orator's guile he says that they *were entrusted with the oracles of God*. 'Oracles' are divine utterances. The Jews were entrusted with the spoken words of God; for their own benefit and correction certainly, no doubt also to enlighten the rest of humanity. Even if *some* Jews *were unfaithful* (as indeed they were) *their faithlessness* could not *cancel* the reliability of God's statements. The very word 'disloyalty' is usable only if there is a previous understanding of 'loyalty'. Even *if all men* (and perhaps women) *be proved liars* they are fighting the truth about human existence as designed and declared by God. Using words from the penitential Psalm 51.4, Paul imagines a dispute between God and his people (hostility to God, hinted at here, becomes important at 5.10); people, as it were, say: 'Wicked we may be but it is God's fault for putting us in such an intolerable position.' But the penitent says to God: '*When you speak you will be vindicated* (shown to be in the right); *when you are accused* (by resentful people), *you will win the case.* The Apostle, like the Psalmist, has no doubts about the unutterable greatness of God (majestically phrased in 11.33–36), nor of standing before God as petitioner and complainant. When we do (this is not *another question* as REB unwisely says) our badness *serves to confirm God's* saving goodness (REB *injustice* and *justice*, but that suggests an employment tribunal). Must we then say, *in human terms*, that God is wrong to bring his anger to bear? But if not, how could he pass judgment on what is wrong in human society (the meaning of *world* here and elsewhere in Romans)? And if he failed to do that, how could God be good?

3.7–8 Very soon the main reason for this long argument will become plain: namely, as a rebuttal of the charge that Paul disloyally prefers Gentiles to Jews. But he now takes the opportunity to wrap up the other complaint, that Paul is indifferent to morality because he refuses to make Gentile converts obey the Instruction. Someone could say, perhaps had said, *If the truth of God is displayed to his greater glory through my falsehood, why should I any longer be condemned as a sinner? Why not indeed 'do evil that good may come', as some slanderously report me as saying?*

That of course deserves contempt – which it does not always receive. In the modern world some use and give support to indiscriminate violence and murder to remedy grievances, or ethnic cleansing to remove threats to national identity, or the destruction of forests to provide income for undeveloped economies, and so on. Such dreadful activities deserve condemnation – but so also do the grievances, the threats, the lack of development that prompted them. When an outrage occurs we speak with horror of the injury to innocent people. But there are no innocent people. They may be blameless, but willy-nilly they are involved in, dependent on, profiting from whatever lies behind the grievance.

3.9–19 Now comes Paul's oratorical climax: *All, Jews and Greeks alike, are under the power of sin.* Here, for the first time, he introduces the word sin which appears again forty-six times (dominating chapters 5–7), not to mention the verb and the adjective. It obviously calls for special thought, but first let him fire off his impressive denunciations. They portray a society that neither begins with an understanding of God or a search for him, nor ends with reverence for him. Standards have gone astray and become debased; kindness is lacking; verbal injury, treachery, venom, and malice lead to violence, ruin, and misery – and there is no way to peace. To us that must sound like a familiar inner-city problem, or civil war in some land that has tragedy enough without bloodshed. But all these words are as *scripture says* (vv. 10–12 from Pss. 14.1–3 and 53.1–3; v. 13 from Ps. 5.9; v. 14 from Ps. 10.7; vv. 15–17 from Isa. 59.7–8; and v. 18 from Ps. 36.1) and they are addressed to Jews. They may be a defensible description of Gentile society too, but scripture indicts Jews *who are under the law*.

Of course the Psalmist does not imply a total absence of devout and acceptable people. Think of Ps. 119 which begins 'Happy are they whose way of life is blameless, who conform to the law of the Lord' and goes on in that strain for a hundred and seventy-six verses. Think of Proverbs 1 where Solomon pictures the evils spread out before his son, and expects him to avoid them. Think of the Pharisee Paul 'by the law's standard of righteousness without fault' (Phil. 3.6). And has not Paul argued (in 2.26–29) that an uncircumcised Gentile who keeps the law will qualify as if he were a circumcised Jew, and that a real Jew, who is inwardly a Jew, is commended by God? Is that not a definition of being 'righteous'? But Paul is talking about Jewish communities and Gentile society when he says *that no one may have anything to say in self-defence, and the whole world* (not individuals from China to Peru, but Eastern Mediterranean society) *may be exposed to God's judgment*.

3.20 Judgment decides what is right and wrong. There are numerous ways of imagining wrong-doing, whether ignorant, careless, or deliberate e.g. making a culpable blunder, disobeying a command, or (the thought represented by *sin*) failing to hit a target. Everyone knows that sin is a religious word: wrongdoing that is offensive to God (though imagining an offended God seems in itself offensive), that shows disregard for God and makes others contemptuous or despairing of him. Paul sometimes uses the plural in that sense (e.g. when quoting scripture at 4.7–8 and 11.27), but usually adopts the singular to indicate not 'sin' (a wrong action that people perform), but 'Sin' (a power to which people become subject). *All Jews and Greeks alike are under ... Sin*, i.e. under its power (as REB correctly interprets). At 7.14 the imagery is explicit: 'sold as a slave to

Sin'. Sin is something like an addiction, it may be to sweets, or drugs, or gambling, or kleptomania – none of which gives satisfaction. In fact, you rather dislike the habit and wish you could stop. The rules you know: eat a balanced diet, drugs only on prescription, stakes you can really afford, and pay for what you take. But the rules only demonstrate that you are caught. *For no human being can be justified in the sight of God by keeping the law: law brings only the consciousness of sin.* Not a remorseful awareness of being sinful, but an unhappy awareness of the power of Sin. There are great benefits of possessing the Instruction (God's *law*) but conscientiously *keeping the law* cannot produce human existence acceptable to God. Paul's formulation is striking and memorable, but it is not original. He found it in Ps. 143 (the whole of that splendid penitential psalm ought to be read, and pondered on). The Psalmist says (in the Greek from which Paul's words are taken): 'Lord, hear my prayer … hear me in your saving goodness (righteousness); do not enter into trial with your servant for no living person will be acceptable (justified) before you' and he goes on to say that an enemy has hunted him down. This is no obstinate sinner but a devout servant of God who needs deliverance from an enemy that ruins all his devotion. Paul names that enemy as Sin, not overcome but highlighted by devout, Pharisaic practice of the law.

So this is the situation of both Jews and Greeks; if people willy-nilly are persistent wrongdoers, God's anger is brought to bear: they are handed over to, no longer protected from, the horrible consequences of what they have done. In that situation, what is required of them? Is it further punishment? Is it humiliation for the satisfaction of the godly? Is it encouragement to behave better and keep the commandments – which is precisely what they cannot do? Or is it faith, reliance on God whose anger is turned against Sin?

The saving goodness of God in Christ
3.21–26

With an emphatic *But now* Paul turns from 'consciousness of sin' to the *righteousness of God*, that is, his saving goodness. That theme, which was introduced at 1.17 (see p. 5) is dominant. It is important to remember that Paul does not regard God as the head of the judiciary impartially administering a legal code. That familiar impression naturally arises because the word 'law' appears sixty-nine times in Paul's Greek. But for him, as for all Jews, the Greek word for 'law' meant at least the five books of Moses which indeed include a great deal of social legislation but also a great deal more: origin stories, tribal histories, encounters with deity, ritual practice and constructions, relations with neighbours and so on. The English word 'instruction' has meanings ranging from teaching and advice to command. Hence the proposal in this commentary to allow it, at least sometimes, to replace 'law'.

The *law and the prophets* indeed bear witness to the saving goodness of God, *but now it has been made known quite independently of law* – namely (and this is the important statement) *through faith in Christ for all who have such faith – all, without distinction*. From this point until the end of chapter 5 Paul will explore the meaning of that statement; but let something be said at once about faith. Since for Paul 'Jesus Christ' always implied death and resurrection, faith is the conviction that Christ is God's representative and the confidence that victory comes only through defeat.

That explanation might still stand if a different translation were accepted. In verse 22 through (our) *faith in* Jesus *Christ* could just as properly be translated 'through the faithfulness of Jesus Christ (to God)'. NRSV puts the alternative translation in the margin, and does so again in verse 26. In a sense, no doubt, Christians may be expected to model themselves on the faith of Jesus but this seems an off-hand introduction of the thought. And Paul's argument from verses 21 to 31 contrasts our practise of the Instruction with our exercise of faith.

To understand his intention we first need a wooden translation of verses 23 to 26:

23 For all have sinned
   and fall short of God's glory
24 being justified freely by his grace
   through the liberation in Christ Jesus
25 whom God intended as an expiation
   through faith
   in his blood
   for a demonstration of his justice
   on account of the overlooking of pre-performed sins
26 in the forbearance of God
   for the demonstration of his justice now in the present
   for him to be just
   and justifying the person who (lives) from faith in Jesus.

That rambling statement, between *for* in verse 23 and *then* in verse 27, is clearly intended to convey serious theological argument but it is not easy to follow the train of thought (because of the puzzling grammatical structure) or to grasp its meaning, partly because of uncommon words. (The word for 'expiation' is nowhere else used by Paul, nor any words related to it. The 'blood' of Christ is mentioned again in 5.9, referring back to this passage; elsewhere only with reference to the Lord's supper in I Corinthians. The word for 'sins' in verse 25 appears only once elsewhere in any Pauline writing. The words for 'overlooking' and 'pre-performed' occur nowhere else in the New Testament.) How is it possible that Paul should present this important section of his argument so obscurely? Possibly because he was making use of an already-existing Christian theological statement, familiar to the Roman community, to which he added his own comments, especially his emphasis on grace and faith. If so, it would be clear that Paul was not the first to give theological importance to the death of Christ, but was building on an existing foundation.

We begin in verse 23 with the problem: *All alike*, Jews and Greeks, *have sinned* – which is more than 'have committed some wrong' by accident or choice. To sin is to take a wrong course, to be fixated on the wrong target. In consequence, human social life is *deprived of the divine glory* – which is a disastrous condition. For Paul human beings are made in the image and glory of God. The divine being who sustains and controls all existence is properly marked by glory. That word could mean high renown or honour, as it did to the Greeks; but to Paul with his Jewish culture it meant magnificence and great beauty. That was how he thought about God – and how he wished to think about humanity. Paul would know as well as we do that human social existence is very often tawdry, repulsive, and shock-

23

ing: we can think of shanty towns, polluting industrial centres, refugee camps, and so on. But there are kinds of glory – music and poetry are good examples – which even God could not display without human minds and bodies. For Paul, all human existence, from its most vast and majestic to its most private and simple, is to display glory – and to be deprived of that is calamitous.

That is why we need God's *act of liberation in Christ Jesus* – in his death and resurrection (rather than in his *person* as REB says) which is an indicator of what must happen to us. We must accept the death of our existing, deeply unsatisfactory life, and allow ourselves to begin a new, as yet unexplored, life – what Paul will later call 'the glorious liberty of the children of God' (8.21). We accept an ending and allow ourselves to begin anew because we are being *justified freely by his grace*. That is, God is accepting us and doing what is right for us *by his free grace alone*. *Grace*, a word of fundamental importance for Paul's theology, is the spontaneous generosity of God to weak, fallible, desperate and often resentful people. It is free people, not enslaved people, who are acceptable to God. Therefore God is intent on setting people free. It cannot be too strongly asserted that God is not primarily concerned (despite references to law and the use of 'just' and 'justice') with maintaining legal requirements that bind both him and us. He is not operating a legal tribunal but a rescue service. Paul works with two structures, law and grace. The law structure defines and punishes sin. Obedient conformity is the basis of social relations, and of religious relations of people to God. People are responsible for their own conformity. Law is achievement orientated (hence the old-fashioned phrase 'works of the law'). The grace structure is dependence orientated: we are what we receive, not what we achieve. Religious relations with God are dependent on God's charity to the undeserving. It demands not achievement or conformity but awareness of need and readiness to receive – and to allow others to receive. The *liberation* in *Christ Jesus* is from law into grace.

God intended Jesus as an 'expiation' – which REB develops as *the means of expiating sins*. According to *The Concise Oxford Dictionary*, 'expiate' (a little-used word) means to pay the penalty for wrongdoing, or to make amends. But the penalty of persistent wrongdoing is, according to Paul, being handed over to the consequences of misdeeds. How Paul understood 'expiation' we cannot know because he made no other use of the word. In secular Greek it means to appease God and win his favour, a votive offering to induce the gods to do what they can do if they so please. Appeasement language regards sin as a distortion of personal relations, to be put right (in the Old

Testament) by repentance, sacrifice, and forgiveness. In Maccabaean times, when Jews were fighting for their national existence against Greek oppression, the 'expiation' word was used of the courageous and faithful martyrs in the hope that their deaths would move God to save his people out of his own compassion. But in Paul's presentation, Jews and Greeks need rescue not from a savage external oppressor but from their own obsessively self-inflicted ruin. In Christ Jesus, God has provided an atonement (a means of setting right what has gone wrong), which is available only to faith and is effected by Christ's death and (as we shall see in chapter 5) his resurrection. The words *through faith* (i.e. in Jesus, as in the next verse) might well have followed 'expiation', but Paul changed the expected order so that he could conclude his unwieldy sentence by indicating the effective scope of Christ's death. It is a double demonstration of God's doing what is right in the past and in the present. REB speaks of God's *justice* (the exercise of authority in maintaining what is right), says that *he is himself just* (acting in accordance with what is morally right or fair), and *justifies* (show the rightness of) *anyone who puts his faith in Jesus*. But that is the sort of language used in, say, an equal opportunities tribunal. What Paul means is that God does what is right, i.e. wise and effective, for people under the power of sin. They must be released from that power with a clear demonstration that *the sins of the past* were indeed not *overlooked*. But once released, they must not drift back into the power of sin. So God himself does what is right and treats as right anyone who lives by faith in Jesus. There is a double demonstration not *that* God does what is right, but *how* his doing right operates, namely by promoting faith in Christ.

Jews and Greeks
3.27–31

Paul now briskly sums up his reply to the double charge of pre-
ferring Gentiles to Jews and of sitting light to the Instruction (law).
What room then is left for Jewish (not *human*) *pride* in God and the law
(2.17, 23)? *It is excluded* – not by insufficiency of performance but by
sufficiency of faith. Any person is acceptable to God by faith *quite
apart from any question of keeping the law*. It is a basic Jewish confession
that 'the Lord our God is one' (Deut. 6.4): so if it is faith for Jews it
must also be faith for Gentiles. Does that mean *using faith to undermine the law* (Instruction)? *By no means: we are upholding the law*
(Instruction) in its original intention.

Before taking up that introductory remark, it is worthwhile
making an effort to transpose the major Pauline judgments to our
own situation. Do we, with Paul, see glory, righteousness (doing
what is right), and grace as describing God as he is? Is he the God
of all people, of Jews and Christians, of other believers and non-
believers? Are we all under the power of Sin, and does God provide
a liberation and an atonement (setting right what has gone wrong)?
And can we claim it not by obeying religious rules, not by displaying
our identity markers, but by faith?

Abraham's faith
4.1–25

4.1–3 To demonstrate the soundness of his argument, Paul turns to Abraham, in whom God's original intention should be seen because he was the founding father of Israel and indeed *of many nations* (4.17). According to Gen. 12.1–3, Abram (as he was then named) was to establish a social community that, in prosperity and adversity, was to be the standard by which all human society would be judged. Why was Abraham so chosen? Was he acceptable to God because of his achievements? Even though the law was not given (to Moses) until much later, perhaps (as Gen. 26.5 says) 'Abraham obeyed me and kept my charge, my commandments, statutes and laws' by inward inspiration. If so *he has grounds for pride* or self-satisfaction over against non-Jews – but not so far as God is concerned. Listen to scripture (Gen. 15.6): *Abraham put his faith in God, and that faith was counted to him as righteousness.*

A great deal of theological enquiry has been given to those words: does 'righteousness' imply moral goodness or a formal verdict of acquittal? Does 'counted' imply that, properly, good deeds were required but that faith was accepted instead so that righteousness was imputed? But the plain meaning of scripture is this: that Abraham's faith was regarded by God as a satisfactory qualification for becoming the founding father of Israel. In Gen. 15.1–5 Abraham was in despair because he had no family to continue his name. God promised him a son and added that his descendants should be as numerous as the stars. Abraham believed God and his faith was the foundation of his family. Faith is thus reliance on God's faithfulness, and the constitutive basis of the godly community.

4.4–5 It can, of course, be taken for granted that Abraham was not only a trusting but also an obedient man (as James 2.21–24 feels it necessary to say). But Paul needs to turn his argument towards non-obeying people, and that he does by pressing home the implications of 'regarded', or 'counted', or 'reckoned'. Remembering that Paul has his eye on sinners, and particularly Gentiles, the argument goes something like this: 'When a contractor carries out his duties, what he receives is not a kind gift but his agreed wage. When a freelance carries out no duties, but puts his trust in him who accepts the ungodly, then his trust is regarded as satisfactory.' That bold, almost perplexing, switch from the illustration to scriptural reference requires sensitivity to the social implication of words. Paul's alert ear picks up the words (in the Greek translation of Ex. 23.7) 'You shall not decide in favour of the godless for a bribe.' The word 'godless' (REB *wrongdoer*) comes only once more in 5.6 (REB *wicked*). No doubt the godless did wrong and were wicked, but to a pious Jew they commonly were Gentiles. This apostle to the Gentiles (11.13) knew that God accepted the ungodly Gentiles when they put their trust in him. Faith sets them in the right position: God does not have to be bribed to *acquit the wrongdoers* who put themselves unreservedly in the hands of God.

4.6–8   An arguable interpretation of a passage from the Pentateuch should, in principle, be supported by a passage from elsewhere. Paul turns to Ps. 32.1–2 where 'not reckoning sin' is equivalent to 'accepting the ungodly'. The whole Psalm should be read and pondered since 'many are the torments for the sinner but mercy enfolds those who hope in the Lord'. Paul has no need elsewhere to invoke the Jewish teaching about repentance and forgiveness for he is concerned with those who may be genuinely repentant but are still under the power of sin.

Paul's teaching that trust in God was Abraham's outstanding quality is well demonstrated – from God's promise to make him into a great nation and his immediate departure into the unknown future in Gen. 12.1–4, to his death at a great age in Gen. 25.8. In response to Abraham's faith, God made a covenant with his people (not a compact, but a promise of divine instruction and support for Israel's social life), described first in Gen. 15 and then in Gen. 17. In the former account, the promise is completed by an extraordinary sacrifice: a smoking brazier and a flaming torch (signifying the presence of the Deity) passed between the divided pieces of the sacrificial animals. In the second account, the promise is completed by the circumcision of 'every male among you in every generation'. The message to Jews is plain: there can be no guarantee of social existence without pain, bloodshed, and death. In Gen. 15 God himself is in the very midst of it; in Gen. 17 every Jewish male has evidence of it in his own body.

4.9–12   So Abraham's faith came first, his circumcision second. Therefore he is the founding father of Gentile believers who have faith to their credit, and founding father of Jewish believers who are indeed circumcised yet *follow that path of faith which our father Abraham trod while he was still uncircumcised*. Jewish practice of the law is not denied or excluded but it is, like circumcision, their sign of faith. It is not anyone else's sign of faith. So for Gentiles, practise of the Law as a religious duty is not obligatory.

4.13–17 But that conclusion could be resisted. Abraham had been led by God to have great expectations: that he would have innumerable descendants, that they would possess the land of Canaan, and that all other peoples would measure their existence by Abraham's standards. It is remarkable how insistently this was asserted – in Gen.12.2–3, 7; 13.14–17; 15.5, 7, 18–21; 17.8; 18.18; 22.18. All these passages should be read in order to savour the longing that the Jews must have felt. In the second century BC Ben Sirach wrote: 'Abraham was the great father of a host of nations; no one has ever been found to equal him in fame. He kept the law of the Most High; he entered into a covenant with him, setting the mark of it on his body. When put to the test he proved steadfast. Therefore the Lord assured him on oath that through his descendants nations should find blessing, and that his family should be countless as the dust of the earth and be exalted as high as the stars; that their territories should extend from sea to sea, from the river to the ends of the earth' (Ecclus. 44.19–21). Perhaps three hundred years later, in the second century AD, a Jewish writer said that the unwritten law was known to Abraham, that the commandments were kept, and that the promise of life that should come after was planted (II Baruch 57.1–2).

Note that word promise. It is not an Old Testament word, nor was it used in Greek life for promises made by the gods. But in Paul's day its use was becoming familiar in Jewish circles, and Paul now re-defines his argument in terms of promise. And for him a promise really is a promise – not the reward of a contract properly fulfilled but *a matter of sheer grace*. It is made to Abraham's descendants in response to their faith in God – not in response to their performance or ill-performance of the law. They are never in a position to say 'We have carried out your law – now fulfil your promise.' If you drag law in at this point, you will know only *retribution* (divine anger); if at this point law is left aside *there can be no breach of law*. Later in the letter, Paul will 'delight in the law of God' (7.23), but here he insists that nothing should come between Abraham's descendants and God's magnificent promise.

Obviously, however, that promise was not to result in Jewish rule over the whole Near East (from sea to sea, from the river to the ends of the earth) – not after the still-remembered revolt against the

Syrian Greeks, and the present dominance of the Romans. Perhaps the Jews were no longer a Near Eastern people looking eastward, but a Mediterranean people. Were there not now Jewish communities in Alexandria, Antioch, Ephesus, Rome – perhaps even in Spain? Was it not possible that the promise was to *be valid for all Abraham's descendants, not only for those who hold by the law, but also for those who have Abraham's faith? For he is the father of us all, as scripture says: 'I have appointed you to be father of many nations.'*

4.17–22 *Abraham had faith in the God who makes the dead live and calls into being things that are not.* Paul was convinced that (*a*) life can succeed death, and (*b*) that existence can be called into being from non-existence. For (*a*) he was doubtless indebted to his pharisaic origins (see Acts 23.8 where 'Sadducees say that there is no resurrection' and Pharisees say that there is), encouraged perhaps by Dan. 12.2, Wisd. 16.13 and Tob. 13.2, and moved to active belief by the resurrection of Christ. Life after death belongs to the essential activity of God. For (*b*) he had the necessary hint in Isa. 48.13: 'My hand founded the earth, my right hand spanned the expanse of the heavens; when I summoned them, they came at once into being.' As in Gen. 1.3 'God said, Let there be light; and there was light.' God speaks, God calls – and there it is! That becomes very important in Paul's doctrine of calling, as we shall see in 9.24–26. We are what we are called to be.

Yet Abraham had to exercise faith when *hope seemed hopeless*. He sharply realized that his own body was worn out, that Sarah's womb was moribund. The promise of a son at their age – not by a secondary wife, but by Sarah through whom alone the divine promise could be fulfilled – was ludicrous. They both laughed (Gen. 17.17; 18.12). Yet *no distrust made him doubt God's promise but, strong in faith*, he *gave glory to God* – that is, said 'You can do it if you wish' – *convinced that what he had promised he was able to do.* Not only that God could do what he had promised ('Is anything impossible for the Lord?' Gen. 18.14; 'Everything is possible for God' Mark 10.27) but that he would do what he had promised. This is not human hope which carries a streak of uncertainty, but hope based on a divine promise which is firm. *And that is why Abraham's faith was 'counted to him as righteousness'*. His utter reliance on God made him acceptable as the founding father of many nations.

We have almost finished with Abraham (he fleetingly appears at 9.7 and 11.1) but something more needs to be said about him. According to Gen. 17.17 he was a hundred years old, and Sarah ninety. (Do not be perplexed by Gen. 25 where he marries another wife who produces six children: these are merely collateral tribal linkages. That they are recorded later does not mean that they took place later.) To us, married couples in the nineties are not surprising (though nonagenarian pregnancies still are); but in Paul's day they certainly would be. Not more than a century later than Paul, life expectancy in the Roman Empire was only twenty-six years. When mortality was so high, God was indeed bringing life out of death when he promised to make this nomad the *father of many nations*. Faith is shown to be reliance on God's faithfulness to his promise, confidence in his ability to create new life when all hope is gone, the source of human community beyond all calculation, and the only way to live acceptably with God.

4.23–25 The significance of God's dealings with Abraham is not properly discerned until disclosed by God's dealings with Jesus Christ. Abraham's predicament, solved by an astonishing birth when all hope was abandoned, is revealed by the Jesus story as an example of death-resurrection; conversely the death and resurrection of Jesus is explained by the Abraham story as a pattern that applies to all believers. Since Abraham provides the explanatory model of the gospel, it is clear that the Mosaic legislation does not (taken up at 10.5). Paul makes the transition by quoting part of a confessional formula:

he was given up to death for our misdeeds,
and raised to life for our justification.

That becomes a little plainer if rewritten thus: 'God gave him over [to death, implied] for our disastrous misjudgments, and raised him [to life] to set us right.' First said, perhaps, by penitent contemporaries of Jesus – the kind of response that Peter wanted when he told the men of Israel that 'God made this same Jesus, whom you crucified, both Lord and Messiah', and then advised them to repent (Acts 2.36–38).

What it means, however, when separated from such an occasion is uncertain. It is memorable but indefinite: in the first line 'for' suggests 'as a result of'; in the second line 'for' implies 'in order to'. Other suggestions can be made, but none is compelling. Anyone reading the Song of the Suffering Servant in Isa. 52.13–53.12 may detect echoes in the Greek translation: 'the Lord gave him over for our sins' in 53.6 and similarly in 53.12 (though 'sins' is not the same as Paul's *misdeeds*). And 53.11 seems to say that the Lord intends to justify the just one who well serves many people. Clearly the

Hebrew was as puzzling to the Greek translator as it still is to us, and the Suffering Servant at most provides an emotional background for the Christian confessional formula. But it is completely certain that the formula, in dealing with putting right what has gone disastrously wrong says that the only way out is by death and resurrection.

All of which may be interesting in its way, but is it really necessary for Christians today to go back to Abraham? Is it even necessary to flesh out the argument with appeal to the Psalms? Yes, for this reason: our Western civilization (in Europe and the Americas) has its roots in our Jewish and Greek inheritance. In the present pluralistic age we show proper respect for other traditions by drawing strength from a critical examination of our own, by sympathetically measuring their responses to the human condition against the benefits and defects of our own. Otherwise we devalue all traditions and allow ourselves to become the flotsam and jetsam of a free-market economy. The Abraham stories belong to the heroic past; the Psalms display the hopes, successes, and desperation of people who indeed believe in God but have no intention of letting him get away with either remote majesty or indifference to his people. The Psalms are wonderfully articulate (unlike much modern Christian practice) and demonstrate how our tradition communicates with what Philo (writing in Greek) would have called That Which Is.

In particular, however, Paul's inter-action with Abraham raises, perhaps belatedly, questions for us. It was promised that Abraham would possess the land of Canaan. What were the dispossessed Canaanites to do? Was God not the God of the Canaanites too? If Christians had really understood Paul would they have dispossessed and killed the native inhabitants of the Americas? Would they have subdued the Aboriginals and Maoris in Australasia – and so on? Come to that, would they have used men, women, and children in appalling conditions in the mines and factories of Britain, and built their wealth on the slavery of countless thousands? These are shameful activities embedded in our Christian history. We cannot read scripture and say 'Whatever happened was right because Abraham expected it'; or learn our history and say 'Whatever happened was all right because of Christian devotion.' With such a record of ancient guilt and present consequences, is there any remedy other than death and resurrection – finding our way of dying to the past and discovering a new sort of life?

But even when reading Paul for our own guidance, we must still pay attention to what he was saying to his first readers.

Peace with God
5.1–5

If by faith in Christ we have been put right with God, there are notable benefits, but it is not clear whether Paul is simply stating them or urging his hearers to claim them. Is he saying *we are at peace with God* or 'let us be at peace with him'? Does he twice say *we exult*, or call on them to do so? Whichever it is, he expects a response – so, 'let us be at peace with God, instead of being resentful and hostile' is his meaning. At a later point (8.7) Paul will say that the common outlook of human nature is enmity to God and his law. Already he has said that affliction and distress are the opposite of *peace* (2.9–10), and has quoted Isaiah's attack on 'strangers to the path of peace' because of their aggression and lack of reverence for God (3.15–18). Indeed, at this point the whole of Isa. 59 is necessary reading. We are like inexperienced children who think of their parents as enemies – if the parents stop them doing what is acutely dangerous, or prevent them from injuring others, or from necessity move to another town, and so on. God may indeed display his anger, but he is never our enemy (8.31). 'Righteousness will yield peace and bring about quiet trust for ever' (Isa. 32.17).

In fact Isaiah's foresight was true: *our Lord Jesus Christ has given us access to that grace in which we now* firmly stand. *Grace*, one of the key-words of 3.23–26, is God's generosity of attention, care, support, renewal, and hope (contrast 4.18). *Access* is a new word from ancient ceremonial in approach to the king's presence. You do not have to wait weeks for an evasive civil service reply, or months for an appointment with your medical consultant, or years for a court hearing – you have immediate access to God's grace. Let us therefore *exult in the hope* (even confidence) *of the divine glory* (of which we are now deprived, 3.23) *that is to be ours*, as Paul will later explain (ch. 8). *More than this*, let us *even exult in our present sufferings* – 'pressures' would be the stock modern word – which remark obviously suggests the possible origin of enmity towards God. Although they had put their faith in Christ they were subject to pressures, perhaps more pressures than before their conversion – 'the sufferings we now endure' (8.18), specified in 8.35–36, attributed to persecutors in

12.12–14. Such persistent hostility might suggest (wrongly) that God is still at enmity with us. That is a genuine problem which Paul does not explain away. Instead, he proposes how to deal with it: pressure promotes *endurance*, endurance results (as it were) in a test-certificate, which in its turn leads to confidence (rather than *hope* which, in our ears, is rather less positive than Paul's meaning). The removal of God's anger does not produce an instantaneous transformation but an awareness of God's peace in the passage from hardship to confidence. *Such hope* or confidence does not shame us in despair (an embarrassment often pleaded against in the Psalms e.g. Ps. 119.116) because *through the Holy Spirit he has given us, God's love has flooded our hearts.*

What could that possibly mean? A more prosaic translation may help: 'the love of God has been poured out in our hearts through the Holy Spirit which was given to us'. 'Heart' means 'will' or 'determination' (as for example 'I hadn't the heart to break the bad news'). The imagery is explained by such a passage as Isa. 44.3 'I shall pour down rain on a thirsty land, showers on dry ground. I shall pour out my spirit on your offspring and my blessing on your children.' So, through the Holy Spirit our dry and thirsty wills are invigorated by the love of God. But does that mean God's love for us or our love for God? Both are important. They are complementary, not identical. God's love for us finds expression in 'our creation, preservation, and all the blessings of this life'; our love for God in reverent and imaginative obedience. The modern view prefers God's love for us: our hearts are so invigorated that we treat other people lovingly as God would treat them. That would be a large and not wholly persuasive claim. It is perhaps more likely that our hearts, having dried up with resentment towards God, have been brought to life (remembering that the Holy Spirit is the agent of resurrection, as we already know from 1.4 and will learn more fully in chapter 8) and renewed in love for him.

The problem of Sin
5.6–8.1

5.6–11   How has the Holy Spirit performed that necessary miracle, 'affirming to our spirit that we are God's children' (8.16)? As interpreter Spirit ('putting the deepest knowledge into words', as Paul says in I Cor. 12.8) explaining how *it was while we were still helpless, at the appointed time, Christ died for the wicked*. At this point Paul is struggling with the words (he makes two attempts to fashion a proper statement). How could he get the emphasis right? At the very time when we were helpless under the power of sin, when we were godless (the same word as used at 4.5) scarcely knowing that we could be helped! It was not as if God was making something good out of a dreadful death, or smartly taking advantage of a bad misjudgment by Jewish and Roman authorities: *at the appointed time, Christ died for the wicked* (or ungodly); and that special time must relate closely to the conviction that one world was ending and a new one beginning (already indicated in 2.7–11).

That conviction gives special force to what is said about the death of Christ. He died *for the wicked*, that is for their benefit. It must demand uncommon resolution to sacrifice our own life to save someone who is innocent, morally good, universally liked; but it does happen – more recognized in the Greek world than in the Jewish. (In Plato's Symposium, dying for the beloved is stressed as a special expression of the unique power of Eros.) The Jewish martyrs, of course, had nobly accepted cruel deaths, in order to pacify the divine anger, and to bring down vengeance on the Gentiles and on renegade Jews. But *Christ died for the wicked, died for us* (that is, us Jews and Gentiles) *while we were yet sinners*. Not like the Jewish martyrs to re-establish faithful practice of the Mosaic law, but to inaugurate a new world for sinful Jews and Greeks. *And that is God's proof of his love towards us*, evoking our love towards him. It suggests a reciprocal relationship between repentant sinners and God. Is that possible? It is usually supposed (for example by translators of this passage) that sinners must submit and take what is offered. Their feelings – of anxiety maybe, or bitterness, or resentment, or terror – are disregarded. It is a remarkable feature of Paul's presentation of sinners that God's anger is directed not only against wickedness in itself but also against the damage done in human lives. *While we were still helpless* – Paul uses the same or related words (usually translated 'weak' and so on) in 8.3, and it heads his own list of misery in II Cor. 12.10. He does not stand aside in apostolic confidence but 'Is anyone weak? I share his weakness' (II Cor. 11.29). 'To the weak I became weak' (I Cor. 9.22).

If God loves sinners, sinners must be won to love God. To make that point, Paul introduces *reconciled* to balance *justified*. Quite apart from anything we do, God accepts us as right with him when Christ says 'These are mine: I have died for them'; and, seeing that quality of love, we are reconciled to God, we are friendly again after painful estrangement. It would of course be possible to say that God is reconciled to us, that he is now friendly and no longer angry, so that reconciliation is a sociable variant for the more legal justification. But Paul had already worked out in II Cor. 5.18–20 how to use 'reconcile': 'The old order has gone; a new order has already begun … we implore you in Christ's name, be reconciled to God!' One cannot imagine Christ's ambassadors hawking around God's precious gifts to surly clients: surely they were pleading with them to respond to God's grace with loving obedience.

That of course would be the beginning, not the end. The argument carries with it an *all the more certainly*. *We have now been justified* (put right with God) *by Christ's sacrificial death; we* shall be saved through him *from* the otherwise inescapable consequences of the divine anger (which should be the meaning of *final retribution*; see 1.16–18 for the meaning of 'save' and 'anger'). We have abandoned enmity towards God *through the death of his son; how much more* shall we be made whole again by sharing his life as sons of God. Death and life are a joint operation: what the sacrificial death of Christ does is to let loose the restorative powers of such dying; and, in Paul's teaching, the social hope of salvation lies in the future (as he says in 8.24–25). But even now *we exult in God through our Lord Jesus, through whom we have now* accepted *reconciliation*. (REB has *granted reconciliation*: you can grant recognition, but surely not reconciliation.)

In this compact section, the benefits of faith in Christ are peace with God (v. 1), access to his grace with the prospect of his glory (v. 2), justification and the prospect of salvation (v. 9), and present enjoyment of reconciliation (v. 10). But Paul has not yet clearly indicated why the death of Christ can justify and reconcile. References to the blood of Christ in 3.25 and 5.9, to his being given up to death for our misdeeds in 4.25, presumably quote words of belief known before Paul wrote. He himself made scanty use of sacrificial metaphors, and he sets down no sacrificial theory. What he did, especially in chapters 5–8, was to explore the significance of sin and death. In those chapters sin is mentioned forty-four times (elsewhere only eight) and death appears thirty-five times (elsewhere fifteen). Paul harks back to the thought of 3.23 that 'all alike have sinned' where (as explained earlier) 'to sin' means not simply to have committed some wrong but to be fixed on a wrong course. As Paul uses the word, Sin is different from 'wrongdoing', 'misdeed', 'disobedience', and 'law-breaking' in verses 15–20; and it merits a capital S to make that distinction.

5.12   *Sin* is a perverse distorting force, like a warp in timber caused by uneven shrinkage or expansion. But this is a warp in social conventions, standards, and habits – such as racism or sexism – sometimes blatantly exploited, sometimes unknowingly followed. To Paul it appears like a parasite on God's power, using it and finally perverting it. *Sin entered the world* (of human social existence). *Sin multiplied, Sin established its reign by way of death* (vv. 12–13, 20–21). Sin can be an indwelling power with its own perverse but persuasive law (7.17, 20, 23, 25), deceiving and destroying (7.6, 11, 13), enticing people into its service and rewarding them with death (6.23). People may be under the power of sin, enslaved to it, whether knowingly or not (3.9; 6.16–20).

It was through one man that sin entered the world, and through sin death. Obviously Paul is thinking of Adam (which is simply the old Hebrew word for a human being) and his banishment from the magical existence in Eden (Gen. 3). When the Lord God permitted Adam and Eve to eat from any tree except the tree of the knowledge of good and evil, he warned them that 'the day you eat from that you will surely die' (Gen. 2.17). Not 'You will become mortal': that they were already (Gen. 3.22), and Eden was well equipped with trees, fruit, and seeds – an ingenious device for coping with mortality. When they disobeyed, the sentence passed on them was a kind of death: the woman enduring the hardships of pregnancy – the birth-pains, in subjection to her husband; the man made to struggle with the wretched earth to provide food, dealing with dust which he himself will soon become. In modern Western life we define death by the moment when physical life is extinct, but the ancient Hebrews included weakness, illness, and imprisonment in the realm of death. For most of them death ended contact with the family and God's people, and separation from God: 'Death cannot praise you, nor can those who go down to the abyss hope for your truth. The living, only the living can confess you' (Isa. 38.18–19).

As Paul sees the human social situation, the perversity of Sin extends the dreadful experience of dying and being dead to *the whole human race*. He is often attacked for having been obsessed with sin, but who are we to deride him when we survey our own world? We see the pollution and permanent destruction caused by modern high technology industry, agriculture and fishery; the violence of endemic warfare and religious terrorism; the personal injury of forced labour, of sexual violence, of torture, of experiments on unknowing or unwilling subjects – some part of this promoted by the economically or politically powerful, some part of it by scientists and technicians, some part by representatives of one religion against another, or even of like against like, some part by exceedingly poor people, desperate to live yet destroying their own livelihood. Nobody should deny the immense and distinguished achievements arising from human imagination, intelligence, skill, determination and courage – but always under the threat of self-destruction.

Paul's over-riding intention is to demonstrate that the reconciliation achieved by Christ is for the benefit of all human beings. Jesus is the prototype of the new humanity, as Adam was of the old humanity. Through Adam, a self-destructive perversity entered human social existence, with the result that mortality (in itself a feature of the renewability of creation) became grievous death – shockingly sudden or long painfully endured, dreaded beforehand and resented afterwards, separating those who loved and pleasing only those who hated. *Thus death pervaded the whole human race – inasmuch as all have sinned*. All of us are fixed on the wrong course: even our best intentions are warped. And that is one way of explaining what is meant by the so-called doctrine of original sin. It takes its name from Adam's disobedience that, in some way or other, affected all subsequent humanity. *How* it did so has been much discussed; *that* it did so has been steadily asserted, and denounced. Always with the assumption that disobedience of a superior's command is wrong, and disobedience of God's command is supremely wicked. But it is now widely recognized that the command of a 'superior' may sometimes be for the benefit of the people commanded but is usually devised to help the commander. People are disinclined, except in an emergency, to obey commands unless they can see the benefit and can trust the commander. We are therefore no longer required to feel professionally shocked at the Adamic disobedience and puzzled by the Divine lack of foresight – free therefore to consider what the story is really about in Gen. 1–3.

In the middle of Eden, God set 'the tree of life and the tree of the knowledge of good and evil', or (as the Good News Bible more sensibly translates) 'knowledge of what is good and what is bad'. The fruit of the tree would give the eater information not about morality but about what was beneficial for life and what was damaging. In the charmed life of Eden, God reserved that knowledge to himself, and everything was provided – for human beings as well as for the animals. But God had created human beings – male and female – in his own image. If they shared the divine intelligence should they not share the divine knowledge – both how to preserve life and how to destroy it? Even, how to preserve or enhance some life by destroying other life – which leads to murder, warfare, agriculture replacing forestry, surgery and antibiotics, and atomic explosions? If this set of intractable problems is Adam's fault, it is like an enormous rift valley right through human existence – until God brings life out of death by resurrection (as Paul had passionately argued in I Cor. 15.20–28, 45–49).

5.13–14   From all this it becomes even more evident that Paul is using 'Sin' in a special way: as a perverse distorting force, rather than in its commonplace meaning of a wrongful act. His critics might well say: You sin only if you disobey a divine command or break the divine law. Not so! *In the absence of law* Sin is indeed present though not identifiable as 'misdeed' and so on. (REB *no reckoning is kept of sin* suggests that nothing is wrong unless there is a law against it. But even the Gentiles knew better than that (2.14–15).) In the long period from the origins of human life to the reception of the Instruction by Moses, death in all its dreadful forms dominated human social existence, including those who had gone astray though not *by disobeying a direct command as Adam did.*

And Adam foreshadows (or prefigures) *the man who was to come.* Symbolically Adam can be taken as the impress (as when stamping out a coin) of all human beings, prefiguring the Adam that was to come. In so referring to Christ, Paul is saying something of the greatest importance about him, far more significant than ascribing divinity to him (which in the ancient world would have been fairly commonplace). Christ was the new and only available prototype of humanity. For Paul, Adam was a remote legendary figure, that is: someone around whom Jewish traditions about the beginning of human existence were authentically related. It was therefore apt to treat him as a prototype, by way of explanation and warning. But Jesus Christ was a person of recent history. Moreover, Adam was a farmer (cattle and crops), not an itinerant holy man (teaching and miracles). Adam had a wife, fathered three notorious children and many others and died at the age of nine hundred and thirty; Jesus was not married, preferred disciples to family, and died before old age. The point of comparison between Adam and Christ lies in their contrasting patterns of human existence: Adam from glory to shame and hardship, Christ from humiliation and death to the glory of resurrection.

5.15–17   The contrast must be further exploited, and this Paul does by using words almost in modern headline fashion. Headlines catch the attention rather than giving usable information. The general thrust of these verses is obvious enough: what Christ achieved is overwhelmingly greater than the disastrous consequences of Adam. But the words used, in a kind of counterpoint, repay examination.

Paul directs attention to the *many* with *so many misdeeds*, that is to human beings in their necessary but deeply-flawed social existence – in which *death established its reign*, i.e. self-destruction is dominant. The representative figure of humanity has been the one man Adam who sinned (i.e. went off course) and was guilty of *wrongdoing* and *misdeeds*. (The word used for *wrongdoing* and *misdeeds* is translated 'trespass' in NRSV: it would be better to think of 'false step' or 'disastrous misjudgment'.) But a radically new possibility is now at hand: the representative figure of humanity can now be the one man Jesus Christ. This is by *the grace of God and the gift that came to so many by the grace of the one man, Jesus Christ*. That does not suggest that God has set up a good role-model, equal and opposite to the bad model of Adam; but that human beings need no longer be dominated by self-destruction but can *live and reign* (i.e. develop constructive forms of existence) *through the one man, Jesus Christ*.

Because Paul uses the Greek word for law when talking about the Mosaic Instruction, because words in verse 16 like *judicial action, verdict*, and *acquittal*, are used together with a word like *offence*, many readers are firmly convinced that Paul has the imagery in mind of a religious law suit. If so, it is a very odd legal system. It seems to produce an acquittal (vv. 16 and 18) which means 'not guilty'. But we sinners are certainly guilty. Perhaps we should not be blamed – because we never had a chance, our parents were unloving and our teachers negligent, we were allowed to watch violence on television … and so on – all the same we are guilty and share guilt with our generation. What sort of legal system treats wicked people with acts of grace and generous gifts? That sounds like rural magistrates dismissing a charge impertinently brought against the local landowner; or a people's court repulsing an attack on the local party boss. And in any case, how significant is a trial and its verdict? But Paul is not discussing a particular legal incident, however important that may be to some person or locality; he is dealing with a life crisis of meaning for all. Its urgency is not of the court room. If you are leading an army patrol in impenetrable, mountainous, tropical jungle, and get your directions wrong, the priority is not thoughts of a court martial but getting back on the right track before everybody collapses and dies. If you run a farm or a chemical factory and have managed to pollute a river by your effluents, no doubt you should be prosecuted and (doubtless after a year or so) tried and punished; but the immediate need is to restore the river to cleanness, and plan to work farm or factory without discharging effluents. Seen on a world scale for humanity, if things have gone badly wrong so that death, destructiveness, self-destruction are dominant, what can be done? First recognize our situation for what it is; then admit our guilt and, relying on the grace of God that comes to us through *the one man Jesus Christ*, receive the gift of acceptance (*righteousness*) with God. Then the absolute dominance of death is broken and we *live and reign through Jesus Christ*.

5.18–19   That is all summed up in a more comprehensive statement than verse 12, not difficult to grasp if set out, not as continuous prose, but like this:

> *It follows, then,*
> *that as the result of one misdeed*
> *was condemnation for all people,*
> *so the result of one righteous act*
> *is acquittal and life for all.*
> *For as through the disobedience of one man*
> *many were made sinners,*
> *so through the obedience of one man*
> *many will be made righteous.*

The *one righteous act* refers to Christ's death (5.6, 8). 'Acceptance' would be better than *acquittal*. What Adam's disobedience did was to put us all on the wrong track; whereas Christ's obedience showed us the way back on to the right track. Adam made us all missing persons; Christ has found those who were lost. The word *many* certainly means not only the specially gifted or chosen few: this is to do with human social existence, not with individual satisfaction. But there is everything to play for: whether to stay on the right track and encourage others – or to make them go missing again.

5.20–21   But surely the right track had been disclosed to Moses! No indeed! already Paul has said that law brings only an unhappy awareness of the power of Sin (3.20), that if you drag law in you will know only divine anger (4.15), and that the presence of law makes Sin identifiable as misdeeds and so on (5.13). Faith is the basis of being acceptable to God, not obeying the rules. Law had a custodial function (as Paul had said more explicitly to the Galatian churches, Gal.3.23). The law, as it were, *intruded to multiply law-breaking* – not to provoke more misdeeds (the power of Sin took charge of that) but to bring wrongdoing into the open and get it recognized for what it is. God did not leave human beings in their desperate plight but added the law to make the situation plain. Grace is the formative factor of human life; law has an instructive and protective role. However great and widespread is the destructive power of sin in human social life, God's grace is more effective in doing what is right for us and in producing for us an indestructible life in *Jesus Christ our Lord*.

Those last four words have a familiar ring from their frequent use in worship, part of a standard formula much used by Paul at the beginning and end of his letters (as 1.7 and 16.20). But here they are part of the argument because they come from Paul's confession of faith (10.9): by God's act Christ is Lord of life (see also 4.24 and 6.23). If we follow Paul's example in referring to Jesus Christ our Lord, we are claiming his power and authority in a new life even though we have to manage as best we can with the old sin-ridden existence.

Paul had great respect for the law (as we can see in 7.12) but it was no longer the be-all and end-all of his relation with God and with God's people. If 'holy and just and good' commandments are given a secondary role, how much more the Apostle's own judgments, instructions, and advice in this very letter! To put the matter more pointedly: when Matthew wrote down the teaching of Jesus in five great blocks, did he present them as instruction to be obeyed, or as stimuli opening the way to faith and the corresponding experience of grace?

6:1–2   When in 5.20 Paul said that 'where sin was multiplied, grace immeasurably exceeded it' he was implying that the further you had gone off course, the greater help you needed to get back on course – or indeed to be rescued in an emergency – like a ship under sail, the chart misread or ignored, being driven towards the rocks. But Paul's critics were supposing the conventional meaning of 'sin', as 'breaking rules', not Paul's Sin (as described in p. 37). So they derided him: 'Let us then encourage sinning, so that even more grace will appear' – as Paul had already mentioned in 3.8 'Why not indeed "do evil that good may come", as some slanderously report me as saying'. Though of course there are some who might say that, not derisively but cynically.

But not Paul! *We died to sin: how can we live in it any longer?* The words *died to sin* or their equivalent are in all the translations, but no one can ever have supposed that they are intelligible English. This is one of Paul's grammatical innovations, at first sight puzzling in the Greek, but not difficult to grasp when we remember that Sin often means 'the power of Sin'. So translate: 'Should *we* carry on under the power of *Sin? Certainly not!* Life under the power of Sin has ended. How can we willingly live under *it any longer?*' This is supported by verses 6–7 where we are *no longer slaves to Sin;* and by verses 10–11 where not living under the power of sin is contrasted with living *to God,* i.e. under the power of God. In 7.4–6 Paul again exploits the thought of changing from one allegiance to another.

6.3–4   Paul can assume that the new allegiance was marked by their baptism, the common ritual for admission to a Christian community. The bodily immersion with its symbolic indication of cleansing and renewal marked the transfer from one body or community to another. (In Romans Paul uses 'body' in both senses – physical body and corporate body – and it is not always clear which is which.) Such transfer from one body to another with accompanying ritual is familiar in ordinary life – for example the transfer from family to school, from school to university, from university to legal or medical practice. Or the transfer from civil life to the army; or from neighbourhood life to gang, squad, or team. Experiences of that kind make particular demands on the participants and separate them from the common life. In fact, that happened to the early Christians, but it was the intention that the Christian allegiance should embrace all humanity.

Admission to the new community implied allegiance to its leader. *We were baptized into union with Christ Jesus* (in Gal.3.27, stretching out his hand for a simile, he had written: 'Baptized into union with him, you have all put on Christ like a garment!'). So baptism implies more than allegiance (which would be the meaning of the more familiar 'baptism into the name of Christ'); it implies participation, in some way or other, in his death and resurrection. Converts were not only serving a new Lord, but their lives were now patterned by his experience of death and resurrection. Baptism was more than the ritual entry to a new religious community and less than a mystical or magical transformation into a new nature (as in the ancient mystery religions). It was the act that initiated the transfer of the pattern of death and resurrection from Jesus to the person being baptized.

Baptism brings the baptized under the leadership of Christ. That is easy to accept if it means the leadership of the risen Christ, but not so easy if it includes the leadership of the crucified Christ. But *by that baptism into his death we were buried with him, in order that, as Christ was raised from the dead by the glorious power of the Father, so also we might set out on a new life*. First sharing his death, only then his resurrection. Clearly that is not intended literally. It is not a call to suicide or martyrdom, to be followed by a miraculous resurrection. But something in the Christian's experience must correspond to Christ's death in order that anything in that experience may correspond to his resurrection.

It is proper to press the meanings of burial and resurrection. Paul is talking of a *new life*, not of the old life restored. The old life – worked out with whatever good intentions, yet always thrown off course by the inherent perversity of Sin – has been buried and finished with. That indeed had happened to Paul's former Pharisaic life (as he told the Philippian Christians (Phil. 3.4–11)), and the skills he had learnt as a Pharisee were now available for his new allegiance. Indeed something similar had happened to the Palestinian life of Jesus: beyond the crucifixion, burial and resurrection, Paul says scarcely anything about the life of Jesus and very little about his teaching. Of course, Jesus Son of God is central to Paul's thinking; later in chapters 12–13 we shall encounter likely echoes of the Gospel sayings, and in 8.15 Paul takes for granted that praying Christians will address God as Abba Father, as Jesus did. But all the time Paul is dealing with what Christ does now and will do shortly. If we say 'But wasn't Jesus a failed Messiah?' (in the most familiar modern meaning of 'Messiah' as the would-be liberator of an oppressed people), we must wait until chapters 9–11 where God's promises are questioned and re-assessed.

But something may perhaps be said about the necessary dying before the new life in Christ becomes possible. We cannot tell people of other countries what to renounce but we can tell ourselves, pointing to our national (or at least English) suspicion of foreigners, making us distrustful and harsh when in control, racialist when at disadvantage. We must renounce doing whatever we want to do, even with violence and aggression, indifference to what others may need or think; and, knowing the risks, practising cheating and fraud (from trivial practices to the highest level) because we can get away with it. We must watch ourselves avoiding contact, lest we get involved, putting ourselves where we cannot hear or be upset by tiresome people in need and distress – and align ourselves with Jesus of whom it was said 'he saved others, himself he could not save' (Mark 15.31).

6.5   Since *we have become* conjoined *with him* in what corresponds to *his death,* so *we shall* in what corresponds to *his resurrection.* Paul uses a word, usually translated 'likeness', omitted by REB, suggesting the thought of correspondence. And in this sentence the REB word *if* implies no uncertainty: if, as is indeed the case, we have become conjoined (a word, suggesting kindred, not used elsewhere in the New Testament) with him and we remain so (as the verb suggests) in what corresponds, in our experience, to his death, so we shall in experiences that correspond to his resurrection.

That rather clumsy rendering of verse 5 is intended to make the reader aware of Paul's feeling his way to express what he has in mind. He is certainly not saying that the former existence, with its pressures, perversions, and frustrations is now totally powerless (as the would-be Christian ever since knows only too well). He knows that Christians do not enter fully and at once into the resurrection life of Christ. He had said to the Corinthian church 'Every day I die', and more than once he told them what pains he had to bear. Later in Romans he will confess 'that there is great grief and unceasing sorrow in my heart' (9.2). Yet he is strongly persuaded that a fundamental change has taken place, that it can be recognized, presented in argument, and pressed upon his readers.

6.6   This is what we know, he says: *Our old* identity was *crucified with Christ* in order to make ineffective the body that belongs to Sin *so that we may no longer be slaves to Sin.* That statement departs from the REB by using a capital S to indicate that Sin is the power of Sin (not simply wrongdoing); by abandoning *the sinful self* for the sin-ridden group; and by substituting 'identity' for *humanity* which is too easily taken to mean benevolence (it renders Paul's word *'anthropos'*, with Adam still in mind).

We ourselves are identified, like it or not, with the community of human existence which, in its variety of social patterns, is astray from God. A Palestinian Jewish writer, perhaps fifty years later than Paul, said that 'Adam was responsible for himself only: each one of us is his own Adam' (II Baruch 54.19). But that unsatisfactory individualism recognizes only part of our human problem, taking no account of social pressures on us to conform, to maintain structural inequalities, and to develop hostility towards rival groups. For Paul, pressures of that kind were behind the crucifixion. For him the death of Christ was the action that destroyed allegiance to the Jewish practice of religion and allowed him to escape its perverse enslavement to Sin. What had happened to him could, in corresponding circumstances happen to others: the old identity could be done away with and replaced by a new identity liberated from Sin.

Paul's Greek actually says 'the body of sin' which REB interprets as *the sinful self*. It is inappropriate to introduce the self (meaning a person as the object of introspection or reflexive action (*Concise Oxford Dictionary*) into the New Testament because it belongs to modern philosophic discussion since Descartes in the seventeenth century. Perhaps it was intended to discourage the vulgar assumption that sin has most to do with the physical body. Yet it is true that the human body could be regarded as a microcosm, a model in miniature, of the social body (as Paul did in I Cor. 12). Hence successful conflict with the destructive pressures of social existence points directly to similar conflict with self-damaging pressures of our bodily life. Nothing should encourage the nastiness of 'public faces in private places' (W.H. Auden), such as is daily reported in the media.

6.7–10 The argument begins with teasing brevity: according to NRSV 'For whoever has died is freed from sin.' REB regards it as a truism *because death cancels the claims of sin*, but Paul actually wrote 'For the person who died has been justified from Sin.' That could better be understood as a statement about Christ, namely: 'He who died has been accepted by God (and rescued) from the power of Sin.' So *if* (as is the case) we have *died with Christ* and thus been accepted by God, we *believe that we shall also live with him*. Paul is not giving encouraging assurances that Christ is with us in all our joys and sorrows, but insisting that we are with *him* in what *he* has done and will do. Verses 4–8 make deliberate use of 'with-words': *buried with, identified with, crucified with, died with, live with him*. (The same kind of thing appears again in 8.17, 29, and 32.) Nor is Paul saying that we can look back to traditional accounts of what Jesus said and did before his crucifixion and so obtain guidance and support (which of course we can). Paul is making assertions about Jesus that put him quite beyond the status of law-givers, wisdom teachers, prophets, holy men, and martyrs, *knowing as we do that Christ once raised from the dead, is never to die again: he is no longer under the dominion of death* – though of course we are. Especially if we firmly keep in mind the larger sense of death common in ancient Jewish life (as already explained on p. 37): good endeavours can prosper, go astray, and collapse; well-planned initiatives can be captured for alien purposes and become hostile. Jesus' attack on mismanagement of the Temple strengthened the hands of the powerful priesthood. His training of a dozen male disciples ended in betrayal and desertion. Even compassionate activities that are beyond criticism, if performed in a sin-distorted social environment, can perpetuate the distortion. The healing of a leper, the exorcism of a demoniac, did little more than perpetuate belief in a deity that could make people untouchable, without restraining demonic rivals. But when Christ died, *he died to sin, once for all, and now that he lives, he lives to God*. That is the Pauline pared-down way of speaking: more plainly, when Christ died, he ceased living under constant attack from the destructive power of Sin; now he lives to make God's power available.

6.11 Now we turn from instruction that explains (vv. 3–10) to instruction that advises (vv. 11–15). *In the same way you must regard yourselves* (i.e. take account of yourselves as being what you now are) *as dead to sin* (i.e. no longer under the disabling domination of Sin) *and alive to God* (i.e. living under the enabling power of God), *in union with Christ Jesus*. That final phrase is REB's rendering of 'in Christ Jesus' (there is no actual word for *union*) which was used at 3.24 for God's activity in the death and resurrection of Jesus, and is similarly used at 6.23. Here, however, it refers to believers living *in Christ Jesus* – a well-marked Pauline manner of speaking. Later, for example, he refers to fellow-believers as 'those who are in Christ Jesus', which REB translates as 'those who are united with Christ Jesus' (8.1). That might be acceptable if taken to mean 'those who are united by their loyalty to Christ Jesus', but we should hesitate before using union-words which Paul's Greek does not supply. It is of course quite puzzling to think what 'living in Christ Jesus' might mean: possibly living in such a way that our spiritual nature (whatever that is) is constantly aware of Christ as now a wholly spiritual being; or more simply, living in the company of people who recognize the lordship of Christ Jesus. When the first Christians wanted a name for their communities they chose *ecclesia*: to distinguish that from Greek civic assemblies they could be called 'an ecclesia in God' (I Thess. 1.1), and to distinguish themselves from Jewish synagogues (another Greek word for a community) they were an ecclesia in the Lord Jesus Christ. 'In Christ' means to be under Christ's lordship. It is comparable to the experience we might have of living and acting with the permission, under the instruction, and with the support of the owner of a large farming estate, or the director of a major research establishment, or the leader of a reputable local authority. Something of that quality is now needed to give meaning to the word 'lordship', attached as it is to sincere but stock piety. In Greek life of Paul's day 'lord' had powerful social and religious significance; whereas Christ, meaning 'anointed', was never applied to persons. Hence to Greek ears Jesus Christ simply sounded like a double name. But not to Jews who were aware that some of their contemporaries were desperately hoping that God would anoint (i.e. appoint) a man to rescue his people, give them power, and set them on the road to dominance. Although there was no commonly accepted messianic expectation, either in Hebrew scriptures or even among Palestinian contemporaries of Paul (such as the people who read the Dead Sea Scrolls), any Greek-speaking Jew would know that mention of Christ/Messiah implied the salvation of God's people. So 'in Christ Jesus our Lord' has something for both Jews and Greeks. For those of us who are not Jews, the lordship of Jesus is primary, though the name Christ should constantly remind us of the immense contribution that Jews have made to the world and their unparalleled suffering at the hands of the world. But whether Jesus is indeed *their* Messiah or not is their decision, not ours.

6.12–15 In what follows it is commonly supposed that Paul is requiring his readers to stop moral abuse of their physical bodies, and that no doubt is part of it and will appear again later. But judgments about bodily abuse are always made in a social setting. Our own sexual practice, for example, is partly decided by law and custom, very largely, however, by films and television, by novels and whodunits, by the tabloid and broadsheet press, by advertising, by the pop scene, and by some forms of feminist, gay and lesbian propaganda. When we take individual decisions, as we sometimes do, we are responding as social individuals. Hence is it not possible that Paul is again using *body* to indicate both a physical body and the social body?

In verses 12–14 'you' is always plural, 'body' is always singular. That makes 'social body' a likely meaning, though REB decides for 'physical body'. An alternative reading would run like this: *Therefore Sin must no longer reign in your mortal* community, *exacting obedience to its improper desires. You must no longer put your members at Sin's disposal, as* implements *for doing wrong. Put yourselves instead at the disposal of God; think of yourselves as raised from death to life, and* present your members *to God as implements for doing right.* In this present age the community is indeed still destructible, either through corporate wrong decisions or ill-judged actions of particular members. But in fact they have the possibility of offering their abilities in community to God to do with them what is right.

The intention of this paragraph should become plain when we

realize that Paul is talking about the end of dominance. Sin is presented as a ruthless master, domineering over a group of people and every person in the group – which is very frail and under acute pressures. But they need no longer and must no longer accept that dominance. '*Sin shall no longer be your master* because you have been set free to offer yourselves and your abilities to God.' Formerly they were responsible to the law: their ability and willingness to keep the law was their only resistance to Sin's dominance. But now they are responsive to grace, and with God's generous help they will resist Sin's dominance.

And of course the law itself may be wrong, or may have become wrong. Who, for instance, would now accept the Mosaic law that prescribed death for both parties to adultery? Indeed, who would so accept it in Paul's day? According to tradition, Jesus himself refused to accept that death penalty (John 8.11). Who would now condemn adultery by married women with no penalty on promiscuous men, though that was taken for granted until recent times? What happens to sexual law, especially the long-established teaching, that sexual intercourse between men and women is allowable only to married partners intent on conception, when physical intercourse is no longer necessary for conception? Or, to make a different point, was Jesus not put to death by legal process? Certainly by Roman law within the authority of Pilate, as Paul would have known; and by Jewish law according to John's tradition: 'We have a law; and according to that law he ought to die' (John 19.7), which Paul may not have known. But he knew that Jesus came under the curse of the law for our sake (Gal. 3.13). It would be easy, though not necessarily truthful, to say that Pilate was a corrupt official and the Jewish authorities were maliciously protecting their own privileged position. But that merely shows that law gives opportunities for corruption and self-preservation by those who operate it. Being *under law* may mean (in favourable circumstances) being under the law's protection; more commonly, under the law's demands which may be pressing and relentless; or at worst, under the law's tyranny. But *you are no longer under law, but under grace.* On first hearing, that contrast suggests replacing a proper legal contract (in taking up an appointment, for example) with a goodwill agreement – than which nothing could be more unsatisfactory. But the real intention is different. Law defines the *status quo* and is provided with ways of maintaining or restoring it. Grace by contrast remedies the deficiencies of the *status quo* and introduces new possibilities. Already we have encountered this innovative quality of grace: in 1.5 Paul speaks so of grace conferring an apostolic commission (though REB hides 'grace' under the word 'privilege'). In 1.7 grace is accompanied by peace, in 5.17 by the gift of righteousness; and later in the letter Paul will set out the gifts of God's grace available to the Christian community (12.6 onwards). What then? *Are we to sin, because we are not under law but under grace? Of course not!*

6.16–19   In verse 13 Paul assumes that we can put ourselves at the disposal of Sin or of God, in order to serve the purposes of the one or the other. We have a limited freedom of choice: there is no freedom to do as we please without obligation. Paul now discusses obligation, in a way that seems strange to us and must have been unpleasant to Greek readers, in terms of slavery. He knows the risk, of course (*to use language that suits your human weakness*), but he has good reasons. The ancient world depended on slavery. It is estimated that the population of Corinth, from where Paul was writing, comprised a third slaves, almost a third freed slaves, and the rest free persons. It is probable that the majority of the Roman Christians were slaves and freed slaves. So Paul was speaking to their condition and (in contrast to Greek sentiment) introducing the Semitic conviction that to regard yourself as a slave in the service of a reputable and generous lord was an honour, not a disgrace. Behind this lies the awareness that those who pride themselves as being free persons, are free because others are slaves – and so are themselves involved in slavery (as our own domestic and world-wide conscience well knows). Even so, Paul cannot bring himself to say that we are slaves of God. We may serve God with slavish obedience, but God is not a slave-master. We may have been slaves of Sin – and slaves is an appropriate word, since once entangled with Sin there is no self-decided release – we may have yielded our *bodies to the service of impurity and lawlessness, making for moral anarchy.* But now, *emancipated from sin* (that is, no longer compelled to follow a misdirected course of life) we have, as it were, *become slaves of righteousness,* we yield our bodies *to the service of righteousness, making for a holy life.*

The change from impurity, lawlessness, and moral anarchy to righteousness and a holy life sounds like indignant rhetoric, probably implying sexual wrongdoing and monastic virtues. But the intention was far wider. If something is impure it is not, through and through, what it seems to be: it has alien elements that make it less acceptable, less effective, more liable to decay, perhaps disgusting and even dangerous. Lawlessness implies not necessarily overt criminality but an unstructured life, lacking dependability; when you cannot rely on standard expectations of recognition and safety for you and your neighbours – in fact, moral anarchy. From all that, says Paul, you have been delivered, and firmly handed over to the service of doing what is right as a matter of dedication or (perhaps) consecration. As REB indicates in verse 19, Paul here uses a 'holiness' word; and the translation probably means 'life among the people of God'. In his letters Paul often refers to 'the holy people' (formerly translated 'saints' but in REB, very properly, 'God's' people; e.g. 1.7). 'Holiness' is one of the words used to express the sense that God really is God and not a bundle of natural phenomena or a convenient human myth (it includes his enormous unapproachability and his equally intense attractiveness). Holiness is thus attached to God's Spirit, to God's law and commandments, sacrifices, and scriptures; and particularly to the people who acknowledge him and are called to do his work. In verse 19 Paul uses an uncommon holiness word implying the act of making holy: so translated 'making for a holy life'. NRSV has the old-fashioned word 'sanctification'. 'Dedication' is better, if it implies that people are offering themselves to God's work of saving goodness, or 'consecration' if it implies that God is accepting their offer.

That was possible, says Paul, because *you have yielded wholehearted obedience to that pattern of teaching to which you were made subject*. It sounds like an approved syllabus of instruction that teachers were obliged to use when preparing converts for baptism. What it really means, of course, is that the converts were made subject to a pattern that taught them how to transfer their loyalty from Sin to God. The word for pattern has already been used of Adam in 5.14 who 'foreshadows the man who was to come'. Here it is surely probable that the pattern intended is the death and resurrection of Christ. It is true that the Roman Christians had received teaching (16.17), and that Paul encouraged those with the gift of teaching to use it (12.7); but just as Jews possessed the embodiment of truth and knowledge in the law, so Christians possessed that embodiment in the crucified and risen Christ.

6.20–23   This paragraph is a before-and-after summary. *Before* your conversion you were *slaves of Sin*, caught up (whether you approved or not) in damaging activities (as described on p. 50), free only from the necessity of doing what is right. And what advantage was that to you – now that you are ashamed of what you did? The result of such behaviour is destruction. *Sin* – a savage task-master – *pays a wage, and the wage is death*. Paul may have in mind the words of Isa. 28.14–22 about rulers who have made a treaty with death, who have taken refuge in lies and sheltered behind falsehood – as applied to contemporary life in the Roman imperial system. He was not indifferent to the benefits of that system, and in chapter 13 would encourage a measured confidence in 'the existing authorities', in view of 'the wickedness of men and women who in their wickedness suppress the truth' (1.18–32; the destructiveness of Sin i.e. the pressures of a social system on the wrong lines, would later be displayed with tragic energy by John in Revelation). We ourselves might reflect on our own social system that maintains prosperity by making and selling anti-personal mines, and produces plentiful cheap food by disastrous interference with the food chain.

But now, after your conversion, you are *freed from the commands of Sin*. Instead you are under obligation to God, and that is greatly to your advantage for *God gives freely* (later, in 12.6–21 Paul will appeal to them to make responsible use of their new-found gifts). Their capacities and abilities are to be dedicated to God's holy work, or will be consecrated by him for that purpose (v. 22 has the same uncommon holiness word as in v. 19). The end product of God's free gift *is eternal life in union with Christ Jesus. Eternal life* (already mentioned in 2.7, more recently in 5.21) is life no longer marred by destructiveness. It is not earned or merited, like a good examination result or a grateful retirement pension, but is God's gift – opening out the barely imagined riches of his goodness. Almost certainly Paul has in mind the ending of hostility between Jews and Gentiles. Enmity could be put to death, new corporate life could be discovered in *Christ Jesus our Lord*. Not that such a hope lasted for long or is today evident in our endemic racism.

Consider a less contentious example. In the comment on verse 5, it was said that even for a body of dedicated Christians the dominance of Sin is not totally powerless. We may find ourselves, with the best intentions, doing what is not right. There was a time in our fairly recent history when, a married woman handed over her property and set about obeying her husband and serving him. That we believed was Christian marriage – as missionaries assured people in West Africa. The Akan people of the Gold Coast (as it then was) had their tribal rule for uncles and aunts to be responsible for the care and upbringing of nephews and nieces – very sensibly. But we told them that it was not Christian to do so: mothers and fathers must look after their own children. So to their cost the Akan Christians added parental responsibilities to avuncular ones, with some confusion. We assumed that our tradition of the family was the only possible Christian view.

7.1–6   The before-and-after theme is further explored, taking up the conviction of 6.15 that 'we are not under law but under grace'. For whose benefit does he thus argue? According to REB he addresses *my friends – I am sure you have some knowledge of the law*; but in Greek he said 'Are you unaware, my brothers, for I speak to those who know law …?' That sounds like a special approach to Jewish Christians in the Roman community, whose anxieties about the prospects for Israel will be considered at length in chapters 9–11. They are addressed as brothers, partly because they are Paul's fellow-kinsmen (as they are in 9.3), but also because they are members of a family, 'fellow-heirs with Christ' (8.17). The REB translation *friends* suggests a friendly gathering of interested people, but the interests of friends are different from the concerns of family. What is more, when Paul says that the law dominates a man during his life, the Jewish hearer will know that Paul is doing more than state the innocuous legal principle that the validity of law ceases at death. Most of us (if we are not professionally concerned with law) take the legal system for granted, adhere to it within reason, and for ordinary purposes avoid thinking about it. But for a Pharisee like Paul (boundlessly devoted to the traditions of his ancestors (Gal. 1.14)), the law was a passion from which only death could separate him. How else could a devout Jew, who was not a priest, serve the Lord? He would learn the law by heart so that he had immediate recall of it at any time (and, in any case, cumbersome scrolls of the law could not easily be carried about and consulted). He would study it, ponder its implications, discuss with like-minded students how to understand its obscurities, how to apply it to new situations, how to help less instructed Jews, and so on. A generation or so later than Paul, a famous Rabbi said 'If two sit together and words of the Instruction are spoken between them (in religious duties or worldly business), the Divine Presence rests between them' – or perhaps (taking a hint from Matt. 18.20) 'Where two or three meet together under the yoke of the Instruction, I am there among them.' For Paul that was no longer true. The fascination (which many Christians in their own way will recognize and even cling to, wanting clear-cut moral rules) had gone. In that sense it had died on him and had been replaced by the pattern of living demonstrated in the death and resurrection of Christ, perhaps especially in the Lord's Supper where the dying but living Lord was made present to the lax conscience and the needy spirit (I Cor. 11.17–34).

Has the Instruction then been written off, and has Paul proved unfaithful? No! The Instruction is still there and later will play an important part; but it is no longer applicable to Paul for this reason: he has changed his allegiance from Sin to doing what is right (righteousness). As an example of law remaining valid but becoming inapplicable, think of a married woman, faithful to her husband, whose husband dies. She may (according to Jewish law) marry again without being regarded as unfaithful. For Paul, Sin has died – he is no longer dominated by the former presence of a misdirected social structure – and he is therefore free to develop a new loyalty.

That is Paul making his own confession. In verse 4 he turns again to fellow-Jews in the church: '*So* then my brothers, you *too* have (by God) been made to die, as far as the Instruction is concerned, by means of *the body of Christ* so that you could *give yourself to another, to him who rose from the dead, so that we* (we Jews, you and I together) *may bear fruit for God*. Verse 4 is one of Paul's most teasing sentences, and how you translate it depends on what you think it means. Many suppose that Paul was attempting an argument by analogy: Jewish converts were like the widow who had married again after the death of her husband. They had transferred their former loyalty from a dead law to a living Christ – except that it is the converts that had died, not the law. In that case Paul's analogy is muddled and inept. But such a criticism probably fails to identify what Paul was doing: he was not offering an argument by analogy but turning over in his mind the various implications of death and resurrection. When he was still a devoted Pharisee no doubt an active mind was endlessly given over to the possibilities of 'You must love the Lord your God with all your heart and with all your soul and with all your strength'; now that energy was transferred to 'He was given up to death for our misdeeds, and raised to life for our justification' (4.25).

So, the compressed statement in verse 4 can be put more adequately like this: 'By means of the crucified body of God's anointed saviour, God has made it impossible for you to live any longer under the domination of the Instruction that permits or demands such a death. Instead you can come under the lordship of Christ risen from the dead, and thus we Jews can contribute to God's protective and saving work.'

Then in verse 5 follows a further statement of the before-and-after theme, and a development of it – introducing the notorious pairing of flesh and spirit, though 'flesh' is hidden by REB *the level of mere human nature*. The Greek word Paul uses here, *sarx* is usually translated flesh (it appears in 'sarcasm', meaning flesh-tearing). It appears twenty-three times in Romans. In 2.28 it refers to male flesh, and is so translated. Elsewhere, in an attempt to kill the assumption that *sarx* always implied sexual activity and abuse, REB uses some variant of 'our unspiritual human nature', thus using two confusing words to explain one. It is certainly necessary to choose appropriate modern words: that can best be done if a range of meanings is kept in mind.

Sarx means bodily existence, usually marked by frailty, fallibility, and mortality (often in contrast to God in his power, perfection, and eternity). Thus it indicates our immediate or remote family (2.28; 9.3), all members of our major social group (11.14), and finally mankind as a whole (3.20). Thus Paul's use of *sarx* (flesh), which is basically Hebraic, means bodily existence in a social body of people. 'Being in the flesh' refers to the habits and impulses of Jewish (or Hellenistic) culture. So in verse 5 Paul says in effect: 'When we behaved in the common way of Jewish society, there were wrongly-directed impulses, actually prompted by the Instruction, at work among our members' – where 'members' may mean 'members of our social group' or 'members of our body'. Which meaning Paul intended is not clear; but he may have been remembering the time when he 'persecuted the church of God and tried to destroy it' (Gal. 1.13). When he adds *and bore fruit for death*, he may indeed be thinking of that destructiveness, even remembering his presence at the death of Stephen (Acts 7.58–8.1). *But now, having died to* (i.e. ceased to live under the power of) *that which held us bound, we are released from* (the inflexible understanding of) *the Law, to serve God in a new way, the way of the spirit in contrast to the old way of a written code*. Most modern translations use 'written code' instead of the old-fashioned translation 'letter', perhaps to avoid a popular view that Paul prefers the general spirit of the law rather than its literal requirement. It is, of course, entirely sensible to discover the proper intention of a law (if that is possible) and operate it accordingly, especially if the literal operation sometimes produces unfair or contradictory results. But Paul's intention is different, and it is not made plain by *written code*. Does that imply satisfaction if spoken, not written? And what is a *code*, now that international spy-stories are in decline, and computing has appropriated the word? The truth of the matter is that Paul's 'letter' can mean a bond or promissory note, as it does in the parable of the Unjust Steward in Luke 16.1–8. Faithful Jews believed that God had given them his bond, and rightly so. Already in 2.27–29 Paul had reproached fellow-Jews who accepted that bond without inward response to it. Here he sets the old defensive, separatist assertion of the bond against a new invigoration of God's-bond-with-Israel by means of the Spirit (i.e. the divine Spirit, rather than NEB *spirit*). God's bond with Israel has become too closely confined by the flesh – the habits and impulses of Jewish society: Paul wishes to free it to receive the energy of the Spirit. 'The letter kills, but the Spirit gives life', as he had already written in II Cor. 3.6.

At that point we would expect him to explain about the Spirit, but the explanation is delayed because he needs to say more about the

Instruction. Before following his thought, consider this question: if verses 1–6 are directed towards Jewish Christians in a church that includes Gentile Christians, what can they possibly say to non-Jewish Christians now? Christians today must surely admire and welcome Jewish devotion to God, their respect for God's Instruction (even learning some of it by heart), and robust support for their community as an extended family. Devout Christian groups may recognize themselves in Jewish fascination with scriptural rules and inflexible application of particular laws, in particularism that denies faith and sincerity to groups that revere God differently. Christians, however, must admit that they have outdone their Jewish forbears in mutually destructive inhumanity, especially when theological dispute is allied with a struggle to maintain or acquire power. That is as old as the fourth-century Arian conflict about the divinity of Christ. Today the brutality of Catholic Croats and Orthodox Serbs in Bosnia reflects a breach of communion that took place a thousand years ago. The injustice and violence in Catholic and Protestant Ireland goes back to the Reformation taking place in Western Christendom between the fourteenth and seventeenth centuries.

To all of us Paul insists that our relation with God, with one another, and with non-Christians is based on death and resurrection – not on doctrines but on experiences. Christians should not be surprised and resentful when something they hold dear – and rightly so – crashes. They should be looking for its new replacement.

7.7–13   So far Paul has been talking about communities of people, that is people related to one another in their social activities – notably Jews and Gentiles. With imaginative boldness he has used *Sin* to indicate the distressing pressures in a society that has got on the wrong track; and *flesh* to indicate the habits and impulses of (in his case) Jewish culture. As he will now insist, *Law* (which is of course a social instrument) *is in itself holy and the commandment is holy and just and good.* but operating in a social system that is unholy, unjust and distorted, it cannot remedy the defects. Law in a distorted society helps to keep it going – so there is no salvation by keeping the law, obeying the Instruction.

Paul now turns from society to the individual: first the individual looking back at his experience of a prohibition (vv. 7–13 with verbs in the past), then the individual trying to work out a present response to the Instruction (vv. 14–20 with verbs in the present).

Who is this individual? The question thrusts itself on every reader of this chapter; it has been endlessly debated and has no agreed answer. But there are two or three possibilities. (*a*) When Paul says 'ego' seven times in this chapter he is

point highly personal. We, for example,

medical attention by saying: 'Look – I'm

the practice number, and a deputy tells

come to the surgery in the morning ...' an

the past tense, though a little more easily

e.g. 'One could not have realized the proble

one had not read such and such ...' and s

doing something of that: if so, his argument ...... to any

reader. (*b*) But he may have been doing so ...ing more subtle,

namely speaking imaginatively about human existence with the

model of Adam before his mind. Perhaps the *commandment* in verse

11 was the prohibition of eating fruit from the Tree of Life, so that

sin found its opportunity (the Serpent, perhaps?) *to seduce me, and

through the commandment killed me.* But Adam did not actually die,

though perhaps the expulsion from Eden was a kind of death and

led to a life threatened by death. True, but the commandment Paul

has in mind is the prohibition of coveting (v. 7) from the Ten

Commandments, not the prohibition of eating in Genesis. Moreover

the prohibition of eating was made when Adam was first put in the

Garden; the Ten Commandments were disclosed not to Adam but

to Moses. It is true that Paul earlier connected Adam with the

beginnings of Sin (see 5.12 and the explanation on p. 37) but any

connection between Adam's story and the present I-remarks is more

fanciful than either logical or illuminating. (*c*) Is it then possible that

an obvious solution is the right one, namely that Paul is describing

his own experience, in the past as a Jew, or in the present as a

Christian? But it is extremely difficult to believe that 'sold as a slave

to sin' in verse 14 is the confession of the Christian who in 6.22 is

'freed from the commands of sin and bound to the service of God'.

Nor is it easy to recognize in the admission that *sin found its oppor-

tunity, and produced in me all kinds of wrong desires* the Jew who was

'by the law's standard of righteousness without fault' (Phil. 3.6).

There can be no doubt that Paul is speaking with strong personal

feeling, but his subject is the nature of the Instruction, not his own

moral failings. If Paul presents a discovery (about the Instruction)

that anybody may make, that helps us all.

Return now to what was said before this obtrusive ego claimed

our attention (p. 56). God had given his precious bond to Israel.

From every Jew, that demanded his utmost devotion to God, to his

father, to his family, and to his people. God's commandment was

intended to maintain the life of the community. Any Jew might fail

in devotion, by error or waywardness; but remedies were available

... Only those who knowingly and with determination *... ...* obedience were beyond restoration. For that the penalty was *...sion* or death.

Within that closed system, like many a tribal society, the rules were socially agreed and individually acceptable. But when such a society is exposed to a very different, more powerful and dominant culture, its members can become confused, restive, and (by the old standards) irresponsible. Paul imagines an individual (in our situation it might be an Eastern trader exposed to Western entrepreneurial activity; or a young girl from a traditional home exposed to vigorous feminism) and he gives that individual words to say in verse 9. They may be translated thus: *There was a time when* I lived without the law (condemning or excluding me) – which is more meaningful than REB's odd translation. But Paul's imagined individual is no longer living in a relatively untroubled tribal society but in the stressful Romano-Greek world of the Eastern Mediterranean – in its measure no less stressful than our own world.

What can the individual now make of the Ten Commandments which were addressed to any individual? For example: *You shall not covet.* The old-fashioned word 'coveting' means an obsession with acquiring or appropriating what you lack and think you can get. The Roman Christians would not be unaware of the Jewish Herodian family (see the household of Aristobulus and Herodion in 16.10–11), its relations with the Imperial household, its grandiose spending on public buildings, its sponsorship of gladiatorial combats and public games. In such a world did not the commandment itself suggest that bold coveting could motivate success? Indeed, once you see it this way, the Commandments presume a world in which people (even Jewish people) are unfaithful to God, worship idols, deride God's name, regard no day as sacred, dishonour their parents, commit murder, adultery, theft, lie about their neighbours, and grasp as much as they can. The commandments assume the dominant power of Sin, do something to keep it in check – and thereby keep it going. *In the absence of law, sin is devoid of life* (v. 8) *The commandment which should have led to life* appeared to me *to lead to death* (v. 10). *In the commandment sin found its opportunity to seduce me, and through the commandment killed me* (v. 11) – in effect (a disturbed individual might feel), it destroyed my devotion to God, family, and Israel.

That is something like the shock that comes to people passionately in favour of maintaining law and order if they discover that the order they support is savage and corrupt. *Is the law identical with Sin? Of course not!* (v. 7). *The law in itself is holy and the commandment is holy and just and good* (v. 12). *Are we to say that this good thing caused my death? Of course not!* It was Sin that killed me, and thereby Sin exposed its *true character: it used a good thing to bring about my death, and so, through the commandment, Sin became more sinful than ever* (v. 13).

7.14–23   That is (it may be said) the good news and the bad news about Sin. The bad news is that Sin can use for its own purposes and pervert the good gift of God's law; the good news that Sin is parasitic, has no basis of its own, can only exist by living on what is good. How that might show in individual experience is told in verses 14–25, sometimes described as 'the divided self'. But that must be properly understood. Paul does not imply that his individual is torn between proper and improper desires. This is not the well-intentioned person of weak will, who means to do good but under pressure or through feebleness, behaves badly instead. Not 'I meant to send a donation to OXFAM but spent it on a pornographic video.' This is the person who strenuously does what he thinks to be good, only to find that it turns out unsatisfactorily, damagingly, even disastrously. As one who gives money for humanitarian aid in a violent conflict and finds that much has necessarily gone to the fighting parties, and some to buy cars for international administrators. The divided self experiences a division between intentions and results – as Paul well knew. In his exemplary Pharisaic zeal he did not fall short of goodness, but over-achieved. His zeal for God's law led him to persecute God's church and to become an enemy of God (5.10).

The person in question *agrees with the law and holds it to be admirable* (v. 16), *the will to do good is there* (v. 18). *In my inmost self I delight in the law of God* (v. 22). This is the characteristic feature of the Jewish holy man and the devout Pharisee. Even more it is the posture of the upright man of Hellenistic morality with his *inner man* and *law that my mind approves* (v. 23), who not merely approves but actively attempts the good and rejects the bad. But *when I want to do right, only wrong is within my reach* (v. 21). There are two powers: one he respects and consciously serves – without success; the other he despises and rejects, but does what is demanded. *This means it is no longer I who perform the action, but Sin that dwells within me* (v. 17) – *a prisoner under the law of Sin which controls my conduct* (v. 23). Now that is certainly not the confession of the Jewish holy man or the devout Pharisee, nor indeed of the upright man of Hellenistic morality. They could admit sins and failures, and they did; but they took it for granted that what they did well was good, and that what they did badly could be amended. Paul, however, makes the extravagant statement that *I know that nothing good dwells in me – that is in my flesh – for though the will to do good is there, the ability to effect it is not* (v. 18). The explanatory words are rendered in REB as *my unspiritual self*, which echoes the translation of verse 14 as *the law is spiritual, but I am not: I am unspiritual, sold as a slave to sin.*

The old-fashioned translation (instead of *I am unspiritual*) was 'I am carnal' which usually meant 'lustful' but it could mean 'worldly', i.e. occupied with the necessary affairs of the world – which is a possible meaning of the rather indefinite word *unspiritual*. In the study of verse 5 above (p. 55) Paul's Hebraic use of 'flesh' was taken to mean bodily existence in the social body of people. Any social group may be pressed to defend itself, to gain recognition and avoid hostility. It may go further and be tempted to keep a share of scarce benefits, to advance its claims in prosperous times – and, if given encouragement, to dominate society with its own aims, to make others take the inevitable losses, to put restraints on the weak and encourage the strong. That could be an entirely cynical process, or a 'realistic' conviction that only if the powerful succeed can the weak survive, or a counsel of resignation to take things as they are.

Whatever it is, these are the activities of the 'flesh'. They may include the seven deadly sins (pride, covetousness, lust, envy, gluttony, anger, and sloth), but all are much more damaging when socially organized (as for example, when the press and magazine industry handle lust; when supermarkets and food programmes exploit gluttony – against a background of AIDS and famine in central Africa).

In Paul's own environment there were three obvious social constraints on the individual *will to do good*. One was the publicly inferior position of women (about which a hint has been given in 7.2 and more can be said later); another was the institution of slavery on which the Empire depended, and which helped Paul to travel so freely (Paul's sensitivity to this matter has already been mentioned on p. 50); and a third was the sometimes contemptuous attitude of Jews towards Gentile habits and religion (with which Paul takes issue in this letter).

If the socially inferior position of women, slaves, and Jews is accepted as a natural feature of human life, that becomes part of the meaning of 'flesh', *my unspiritual nature. Left to myself I serve God's law with my mind, but with my unspiritual nature (my flesh) I serve the law of sin* (v. 25). *We know that the law is spiritual*, that is belongs properly speaking to the divine goodness and power; but somehow *in the commandment sin found its opportunity to seduce me* (v. 11); *through the commandment sin found its opportunity, and produced in me all kinds of wrong desires* (v. 8). How does serving God's law become serving Sin's law?

7.24–8.1   That question indicates that major decisions must be taken about *God's law* – they will not be complete until the middle of chapter 15, but the present discussion ends with a cry of anguish from the inmost experience of the devout, upright individual: *Wretched creature that I am, who is there to rescue me from this state of death* (i.e. this human constitution directed towards uncleanness and ruin)? It is answered equally dramatically: *Who but God? Thanks be to him* who deals with us *through* the death and resurrection of *Jesus Christ our Lord. To sum up then: left to myself I serve God's law with my mind, but with my* social entanglement (rather than *unspiritual nature*) *I serve the law of sin*, i.e. the law that enables Sin to exert its pressures. *It follows that there is now no condemnation for those who are united with Christ Jesus.* Because he serves God's law with his intention (which is here and elsewhere the meaning of *mind*, as in 11.34) but is caught up, helplessly it seems, in the demands of his social relations, there is no *condemnation*. That word does not carry the weak sense of 'disapproval' (e.g. 'Bishop condemns lottery') but the strong sense of 'punishment', even punishment by death. For those who are in Christ Jesus, who recognize the lordship of Christ Jesus (explained on p. 48), *condemnation* is replaced by the benefits of his death and resurrection.

Not flesh but the Spirit
8.2–17

8.2–11 Paul now begins the grand finale of the first movement (as it were) of his composition. He takes up his reference to the new way of the Spirit (in 7.6) and to the Holy Spirit that God has given us (in 5.5). He resumes the drive of the argument in 6.1–14 with an extraordinary concentration of references to 'spirit'.

The word occurs twenty-one times (mostly in 8.1–16, with only thirteen more in the rest of Romans). Spirit is contrasted with flesh in verses 4, 5, 6, 9, and 13 (though REB translates flesh as *the old nature*). It is contrasted with 'body' in verses 10, 11, and 13. In verse 15 the *spirit of slavery* is contrasted with the *spirit of adoption*. In verse 16 *our spirit* is allied with *the Spirit of God*: so named in verses 9 and 14. Also *the spirit of him who raised Jesus from the dead* (v. 11), *the Spirit of Christ* in verse 9; and simply *the Spirit* in verses 23, 26, and 27.

So at last Paul is going to talk about the (divine) Spirit or the (human) spirit. (Since in Paul's day Greek was commonly written in capital letters, the modern written convention of S and s was not available to him.) 'Spirit' has a range of meanings: it is itself the Latin word meaning breath. The corresponding words in Paul's Hebrew and Greek are best understood as vital energy. In modern English the most familiar definition (according to *The Concise Oxford Dictionary*) is 'the vital animating essence of a person or animal' – recognizable in such a remark as 'she gave a spirited performance of the sonata'. With that in mind we know what Paul means when he invokes 'the power of the Holy Spirit' to produce abundant hope, or to demonstrate its presence by signs and portents (15.13, 19). But Spirit can seem to be unpredictable (Jesus compared it to the wind, John 3.8), its consequences variable indeed: contrast 'God has infused them with a spirit of lethargy' (NJB translation – properly rendered 'God has dulled their senses; 11.8), with 'aglow with the Spirit' (12.11). There is a spontaneity about Spirit, not to be confused with mere impulse. Not 'I will act as the Spirit moves me' if that implies taking no thought of likely consequences, paying no heed to sensitivities. Paul points to 'justice, peace, and joy, ' inspired by the Spirit (14.17), and commends 'the love that the Spirit inspires'

(15.30). That is to say, the work of the Spirit is not chaotic but constructive.

That is why (at first sight surprisingly) he begins his theme in chapter 8 with *the law of the Spirit* that *has set you free from the law of sin and death.* Has he not just said that 'we are released from the law, to serve God in a new way of the spirit in contrast to the old way of the written code' (7.6)? More than once his argument includes such words as 'apart from the law' (3.21, 28; 6.14, 15), so that his opponents derided him as indifferent to sin (3.8) But they had not understood that the law, in itself good, may become perverse in a corrupt situation. The rule of law means that social life has a structured, not a chaotic, existence. Thus *the law of the Spirit* means the structured existence prompted by the life-giving Spirit of God. Social structures may preserve injustice or may encourage freedom, they may protect antique responses or permit new developments. Paul asserts that *in* (the death and resurrection of) *Christ Jesus the life-giving law of the Spirit has set you free from the law of sin and death,* namely the social structure that is badly astray, destructive, and deadly.

But who is referred to by the word *you*? In Paul's Greek it is singular – 'thee' in old-fashioned English; though the AV has 'me', and so have several modern translations, including the translation into modern Greek. The variation was already present in ancient manuscripts. The significant point is this: in a part of the letter where Paul is dealing with human social existence, he does not ignore personal response – thee and me, and every one of us. And one further thought: if the Spirit has set us free, the words of 7.17 ('sin that dwells in me'), 7.23 ('the law of sin that controls my conduct') and 7.25 ('I serve the law of sin') can scarcely apply to us.

In verses 3–4 Paul states his main conviction about flesh and spirit and then (in verses 5–17) writes his own commentary on what he has said. Clearly flesh and spirit are contrasted, in line with the standard biblical assumption that flesh is weak and fallible, spirit is strong and reliable. But the argument will be totally misunderstood if we give it the common individualistic interpretation and assume that flesh refers to bodily appetites and spirit to mental or religious aspirations. To interpret 'flesh' in terms of human nature is only appropriate if we remember that we are social creatures and invariably behave in line with social pressures or in attempted defiance of them. When Paul talks about 'flesh' he means something like our own flesh and blood, the community to which we belong, the group that defends its interests against all comers and seeks to dominate, or weaken, or revile other groups. Of the varied possible meanings of 'spirit' Paul here relies on resurrecting power (*the Spirit of him who raised Jesus from the dead* (v. 11), made available for a moribund community of people. In answer to the question 'Can these bones live?' God said 'I shall put my spirit into you and you will come to life, and I shall settle you on your own soil, and you will know that I the Lord have spoken and I shall act' (Ezek. 37.1–14). Though with this difference, that for Paul the new-creating power of the Spirit or (as he surprisingly put it in verse 2) *the law of the Spirit*, is available for both Jews and Gentiles.

Those considerations lie behind verses 3–4 where Paul's compressed language needs expansion and some guesswork. *What the law could not do* was to provide a satisfactory (i.e. righteous), structured existence for Jews and Gentiles. *Human weakness robbed it of all potency* (or 'weakened by the flesh' NRSV): it was weaker than the self-preserving drive of Jewish society, weaker than the self-regarding pressure of Hellenistic society. *What the law could not do ... God has done: he has passed judgment against sin within that very nature* (which phrase we shall deal with later: NRSV has 'he condemned sin in the flesh').

How has God done that? *By sending his own Son in the likeness of our sinful nature. Sinful nature* is REB-speak for 'flesh', namely our sin-ridden existence. The word *likeness* can imply similarity or identity: here it indicates identity. The situation in which the Son had to work was the same as ours. He was not dealing with our problems from outside but experiencing social existence like any one of us. Unlike us he was God's *own* Son, that is God's appointed representative who acts with God's full authority, and he was sent *to deal with sin*. The word 'sent' means instructed to go and carry out a particular task: it does not mean that a supernatural being was sent from heaven. In John's Gospel it may be different, but in Paul it has that stock meaning, e.g. 'You are to go to whatever people I send you, and say whatever I tell you to say' (Jer. 1.7). There is a well-known illustration in the parable of a vineyard owner who sent a servant, then a second servant to collect his dues. But when the tenant-workers refused to respond the owner said 'I will send my beloved son; perhaps they will respect him'. The servants are the prophets, the son is Jesus, and the son's task was *to deal with Sin*.

Some translations say 'to be a sacrifice for sin' (Jerusalem Bible) on the grounds that Paul's phrase 'concerning sin' appears often in Old Testament instructions about the Temple sacrifices. But in those passages the sacrificial meaning is made plain by reference to the required animals and procedures, and in any case Jewish religion did not approve of human sacrifice. And the most serious objection to the sacrificial interpretation is that sacrifices may make atonement for sins but do nothing to remove sinning. It is scarcely to be expected that Sin could be prised from its tenacious hold on 'the flesh' by a cultic sacrifice intended to please God, not to dislodge Sin. By the death of Christ God has done more than provide an atoning sacrifice: he has passed judgment on Sin. Sin is condemned to be dispossessed, to be driven out of its apparently impregnable hold on human society. Human social structures are not inherently wicked, but they are so weak, fallible and corruptible that Sin can easily take them over and find there a secure base of operations. The effect of God's action in Christ is to make Sin's position untenable if people will use their newly-given freedom to fight Sin. God sent his own Son to 'belong to wicked mankind, to the company of unjust flesh' (using a quotation from the Dead Sea Scrolls). Hence he would be subject to death and to the perversion of his best intentions, entrapped by sin like all human beings. That does not imply that he sinned by choice or by carelessness or by a defect of temperament, but it recognizes the conviction that Sin exists by perverting what is good and strengthens its hold by destroying what is best.

So then God has passed judgment against Sin by the death and resurrection of his Son – the death demonstrating the parasitic destructiveness of Sin, the resurrection displaying Sin's inability to destroy God's *life-giving law of the Spirit*. What the law was intended to achieve is now fulfilled by us as we are directed by the Spirit.

In verses 5–11 Paul draws out a contrast between two sorts of human association. One, signified by flesh is self-defensive, inward-looking, aggressive, basically destructive and self-destructive. It is law-bound (as in 4.14) yet regards God as a demanding, intrusive presence, and so is at enmity with him. By contrast the community signified by Spirit is self-giving, outward reaching, basically life-renewing and self-discovering. It is a community of faith (as in 4.16) and regards God as the source of saving goodness. Paul sets this out in rhetorical fashion:

5   Those who live in the manner of flesh
     are intent on the flesh;
     those living in the manner of Spirit
     are intent on Spirit.

6   For the flesh is intent on death;
     the Spirit on life and peace.

7   Hence the intent of the flesh is hostile to God
     – for it is not subject to God's law,
     indeed cannot be.

8   Those who live in the flesh cannot please God.

9   You, however, are not in the flesh
    but in the Spirit,
        if indeed God's Spirit is at home among you.
    If anyone has not Christ's Spirit
        that person is not his.
10 But if Christ is among you,
        though the body is dead because of Sin,
    the Spirit is life because of saving goodness.
11 If the Spirit of him who raised Jesus from the dead
    is at home among you,
        he who raised Jesus from the dead
    will bring to life your mortal bodies
        through the Spirit at home among you.

Response to Paul's rhetoric, however, is hampered by uncertainty about the meaning he attaches to 'flesh'. (See the discussion of that word on p. 54). NRSV leaves the word as it is, and that suits well enough *your mortal bodies* in verse 11. But how could Paul possibly say in verse 9 'You, however, are not in the flesh' (neatly avoided by NEB)? Clearly 'flesh' is being made to carry a special sense for which no obvious word can be found in translation. Most modern translations use the word 'nature', perhaps in the sense of 'inherent impulses determining character or action' (*Concise Oxford Dictionary* 7). So, our old, unspiritual, disordered, sinful, earthly human nature – giving the impression (perhaps unintentionally and quite wrongly) that human nature is wholly devoid of greatness and splendour. It is better to retain the awkward word 'flesh' and remember that it signifies a self-regarding and self-destructive way of living in community.

Such a life-style is hostile to God, contrary to God's intention in the Instruction, and never reconcilable to it (v. 7). The trouble with those who are intent on the flesh is that they *cannot please God* (v. 8). Many of them certainly try, but they suppose that to please God they must act by a set pattern of rules and thereby maintain God's authority, even support or defend it. But God's pleasure is not of that kind. It is akin to the delight of a parent observing the growth and self-discovery of a child; or the satisfaction of a teacher when a pupil begins to enjoy learning; or the excitement of a scientist when a research assistant makes a genuinely new discovery; or the relief of a GP when a patient responds to treatment. God is pleased when we are innovative, when we are open to other people, when we discover other kinds of people beyond the defensive boundaries of our in-group – our 'flesh'.

But in the Spirit we are confronted with *life and peace* (v. 6). In developing that conviction Paul uses death and resurrection language in perplexing fashion. When he says *the body is dead because of Sin* (v. 10), what body does he mean? Obviously it is not the body of any individual Christian that has been put to death and raised to life. Not literally, not even metaphorically as, for example in baptism (6.3). *Body* must be taken in the corporate sense: the body of people, either Jews or Gentiles, whose corporate existence had been ruined and destroyed by Sin. Now their community has been given new life (not simply revived) by the permanent, constitutional indwelling of the Spirit of him *who raised Christ Jesus from the dead.* Jewish and Hellenistic social structures were permeated by Sin, humanly unjust and offensive to God. They were *mortal bodies*, but resurrection (in Paul's transferred sense) could happen to them if the life-giving Spirit were at home among them corporately – and individually (*anyone who does not possess the Spirit of Christ does not belong to Christ* (v. 9). And this transformation became possible not through the good deeds of the persons concerned but through the saving goodness of God (v. 10).

Return now to the conviction in verse 6 that the Spirit is intent on life and peace – where God's life-giving activity is matched by our peace-making response. The Spirit is the power of Deity to bring new life out of disaster, *who raised Jesus from the dead.* The *Spirit of Christ* is the Spirit that impelled Christ to accept death, that brought him again from the dead, and is at home among those who are his. Paul is not presenting trinitarian doctrine but he finds himself speaking of Deity in a triune manner. As for peace, it would be entirely in character if Paul had in mind something like 'well-being'; but here it stresses the ending of our hostility to God (as at 5.1, 10; see p. 33; God is the God of peace 15.33 and 16.20).

Paul's use of death and resurrection language corresponds to his conviction that a major restructuring of life in his world was about to take place. That being so, the Spirit would bring new *life* to replace the disintegrating communities – as well as *peace*: the willingness not to resent the changes. We ourselves are remote from Paul's perceptions and cannot judge whether his prophetic judgment was well founded. But in our own day, this post-modern age presses us 'to reconsider the nature of cultures and institutions, the basis of our gender, family and collective identity, the question of society's long-term direction and prospects' (M. Bradbury). Even if those demands are now standard commonplaces, ought not the Christian churches to be responding to the *indwelling Spirit*. To not-unsympathetic observers they seem to be expressing their convictions in a manner devised before the modern world began, offering expectations that ignore what has now become possible, even to be re-inventing the past and promoting it with modern communication techniques.

8.12–17 But, it may be asked, are we not under an obligation to support, defend, improve our community? Since our community offers every family a status and a role to play, since it gives us a tradition to remember and a prospect to encourage us, are we not *obliged to live in that way*? No! That is the certain way to destroy the community. But *if by the Spirit* we destroy the self-centred activities (*base pursuits* was a leaden NEB invention) of our community, then we will discover a new prospect of life.

Paul makes constant use of conflict imagery, and presents an image of people fighting against ruthless and subtle enemies, hampered by natural but suborned allies. Sin is the chief enemy, whose greatest triumph is to make us enemies of God. Flesh is the natural condition of mankind. In itself it disposes of no great power ('all flesh is as grass' Isa. 40.6): it is dependent, always subject and fallible (as in the modern catch phrase 'We're only human!'). How persons of flesh actually behave depends on the activities of their bodies or the bodies they belong to. In verse 13 Paul switches from 'flesh' (NEB *our old nature*) to '*body*'. He turns from general considerations offered by the Hebraic use of 'flesh' to more particular responsibilities offered by the Greek use of *body* (which has no corresponding equivalent in Hebrew scriptures). We are under obligation to the bodies we belong to for what our bodies do.

That obligation is described in Paul's language as the responsibility of sonship: *All who are led by the Spirit of God* – perhaps 'carried away by the Spirit' – *are sons of God*. Not a cautious calculation of what might be useful or correct, not a limited application to the members of a particular group; but *all* who are effectively moved by the Spirit are members of God's family and, in mutual support, share its benefits and responsibilities.

For the first time in the letter, Paul speaks of Christians as *sons of God*, though in verses 16–17 they are *God's children*. In verse 19 the created universe eagerly awaits the disclosure of *God's sons*, though in verse 21 they become *the children of God*. Modern translations, sensitive to the demand for inclusive language (e.g. NRSV), tend to replace 'sons' by 'children'. But since the commonest modern meaning of 'children' is 'young human beings below the age of puberty' (so says *The Concise Oxford Dictionary*), God seems to be presiding over a kindergarten. This is no easy problem for translators. Paul often calls his readers 'brothers': REB says 'friends' (see p. 53 on

7.1) but keeps 'brothers' in 9.3 (NRSV says 'my own people'). Perhaps it would be best to speak of 'the family of God', even if nowadays the family as a necessary institution is greatly questioned. That questioning, of course, could find support – of a kind – in Paul's' rejection of 'the flesh'.

In our generation which has heard, and perhaps taken to heart, the feminist protest against many indications of the exclusion of women, we need help to understand why Paul in Romans does not say 'sons and daughters of God' as he does in II Cor. 6.18 when describing the community that God loves. In the life of his day, Jewish mothers gave the family its Jewishness, whereas men were expected to support its standing in the community, defend it against attack, and improve its prospects. Men therefore were the public, even the aggressive, representatives of the family, or the kinship group, or the community. Hence they needed to know, more than any one else, the different responsibilities of sons in the new community created by the Spirit.

In the old community of the 'flesh', dominated by Sin, they had played out their role in life always on the edge of fear, like administrators promoted just beyond their ability. They feared the success of rivals in the community, the silent disapproval of their mothers and wives, the disappointment of their extended families. If they were Jews they feared the pervasive uncleanness of Gentiles; if Gentiles they feared the perverse oddity of Jews. That was no better than a life of slavery – but not now for Christians (hence Paul's hesitant use of slavery language in 6.18–19) for they had received a Spirit (perhaps at baptism, 6.4) which would see them through the difficulties of life because God's love had flooded their hearts (5.3–5). It was a Spirit that made them adopted members of God's family – though with no diminution of the demand for obedience.

In the earlier letter to the Galatians Paul had already worked out this theme of adoption (Gal. 4.5–6, though REB does not show the connection). *Adoption* was a Greek and Roman institution, but not Jewish. It confers a present status and expects a future inheritance – as for example an adopted child may become an acknowledged member of the family, looking forward to a share in the family property, a job in the family business, and so on. Paul distinguishes between adopted sons and God's own Son (8.3 and 32). He is telling his Jewish readers that they have no more inherent claim on God for preservation and all the blessings of this life than have the rest of humanity. Indeed in 9.4 he plainly says that Jews are adopted children (though again REB conceals the reference). What makes the Jewish people special is not their sonship but their share of the family property and their job in the business of God's family. But all Christians receive *a Spirit of adoption, enabling them to cry 'Abba! Father'* (v. 15).

Abba means 'father' in Aramaic, the every-day language, at all levels, of Jewish people in the time of Jesus – and different from Hebrew which had become the formal language of Temple worship. When Jesus taught his followers how to pray, he began with the single word 'Father' (according to Luke 11.2), which in Aramaic was 'Abba'. He himself thus addressed God in Gethsemane, according to Mark 14.36 which adds the Greek translation pater. And Paul assumes that Abba pater will be familiar to Christian worshippers in Asia Minor and Rome. The implication is this: that in worship at least, belief in God our maker is to be put in our own language, though it is to be founded on Jewish understanding of God's father-hood (not for example on Greek stories of divine paternity – or, come to that, on Victorian models or our present confusion about parental roles); and that we lose the full benefits of worship unless it includes more than one language (or, shall we say?, tradition of devotion).

The Spirit enables *us to cry 'Abba! Father'*. That means 'cry out', even 'shout'. It may suggest noisy, ecstatic worship, but that depends on local tradition: it should not be assumed that God is deaf. Imagine that you are arriving late at night, dead tired, after a dreadful, long-delayed air flight – and just as you reach the barrier, who do you see? 'Father!' you shout. Somewhat like that, Paul's *Abba* is a cry of Christian relief and confidence. There is no evidence that Gethsemane would be in the reader's mind, but such a thought would be suited to verse 17, to which we can now move.

Although Paul mainly speaks about God's Spirit in verse 16, he now refers to the human spirit (as he earlier did at 1.9) – a popular way of talking about our vitality as human beings (see the description of Spirit on p. 62 as vital energy). In that simple sense, human beings are spiritual beings, like the 'birds in the sky' that Jesus talked about (Matt. 6.26). Simply as God's creatures we can expect no more care and attention from the Creator, and indeed no less, than they receive. But *The Spirit of God affirms to our spirit that we are God's children; and if children then heirs, heirs of God and fellow-heirs with Christ*. We can indeed use our human vitality to become social animals, more inventive and destructive than any others. But the Spirit says to our spirits that we are adopted into God's family and therefore have great expectations (in the traditional phrase). In fact, as Paul has already said in 5.17 we 'live and reign through the one man, Jesus Christ'. That is, we have a share in God's reign: indeed, contribute to it in ways that God makes possible to the human

spirit and not to any other being. One might have in mind speech
and language, poetry and music, mathematics and science. So then,
*fellow-heirs with Christ; but we must share his sufferings if we are also to
share his glory.*

Present suffering and final glory
8.18–39

8.18–22   Paul speaks of *the sufferings we now endure*. The word *now* is very important to him. He has already said that God demonstrates 'his justice *now* in the present' (3.26) and that recently 'at the appointed time, Christ died for the ungodly' (5.6). He will later say that 'this is the hour of crisis: it is high time for you to wake out of sleep' (13.11). Since God is marked by brightness and splendour, human beings (made in the image of God) should reflect that brightness, and God's creation should display his splendour. That will indeed happen, but the present is a time of agonized suffering – which Paul expresses dramatically by the groaning of *the created universe* (vv. 19–22), of Spirit-filled Christians (vv. 23–25), and even of the Spirit itself (vv. 26–27).

The total situation is at present gloomy but at no point without hope. Thus *the whole created universe in all its parts groans* (that is the bad news) *as if in the pangs of childbirth* (something new is to be born, so that is the good news). *It was made subject to* futility (rather than *frustration*, which hides the Old Testament reference) but *with the hope* (meaning confident expectation) that *the universe itself is to be freed from* unavoidable ruin. (Paul wrote 'enslavement to destruction': *shackles of mortality* is inept rhetoric from NEB.) Paul looked out on the world where in his travels he had suffered much, and he saw disheartening futility. The creation was not inherently stupid: it was made by God and declared good. So – as others in his day were saying – God himself had subjected it to futility. In a sense, that thought is as old as Gen. 3.17–19 where Adam is told: 'On your account the earth will be cursed.' Food growing will be unceasingly hard work, hampered by thorns and thistles – which by our modern standards is a very modest hindrance. We can now see the destructive effects of social misjudgments and wickedness: the desert advancing in formerly fertile areas, the destruction of forests and consequent loss of soil, the industrial pollution of living space, and so on. It could be said that the creative environment has been put under a blight and that the Creator has made us take the results of our decisions. Perhaps so; but is not the Creator responsible for earthquakes, volcanic eruptions, storms, floods, extremes of heat and cold? Listen to the Speaker, whose book Ecclesiastes was much in the minds of Paul's contemporaries: 'Consider God's handiwork; who can straighten what he has made crooked? When things go well, be glad; but when they go ill, consider this: God has set the one alongside the other in such a way that no one can find out what is to happen afterwards. In my futile existence I have seen it all, from the righteous perishing in their righteousness to the wicked growing old in wickedness' (Eccles. 7.13–15).

Paul responded differently: *the created universe is waiting with eager expectation for God's sons to be revealed*. When human beings are set free from their enslavement to wickedness the consequent liberation of at least the living world from exploitation and ruin must follow. The children of God are neither labourers nor tenants but heirs – and therefore take care of their inheritance, however difficult and demanding it sometimes turns out to be.

8.23–25   For human beings are not free spirits but created, social beings, and they experience suffering – even though they have *the Spirit as the firstfruits of the harvest to come*. Or perhaps 'even though they have the firstfruits of the harvest that the Spirit will abundantly produce'. Paul is urging caution and realism. Early promptings of the Spirit, like the first fruits of the harvest, are to be offered to God: they are not endlessly available for religious excitement. *We look forward eagerly to* (the full consequences of) *our adoption*, namely becoming heirs with a wonderful and demanding inheritance – or, as Paul actually says: 'the liberation of our body'. REB says *our liberation from mortality*, which seems to imply that our physical bodies need never die. What Paul surely means is that the full consequences of our adoption promise free scope for our corporate life. He has in mind somebody who says *We were saved*. This is the only place in the primary Pauline writings where *save* is spoken of as past (it is usually future). Paul does not for a moment deny that the great saving act is done; but we were saved (by God) in expectation that other consequences would follow and be developed. *It was with this hope that we were saved* (*The Concise Oxford Dictionary* defines 'hope' as 'expectation and desire combined'); and in Paul's presentation of the Christian life, expectation is of the essence. If Christians are content to see what they have always seen, they have given up whatever it is that prompts them to *look forward eagerly and with patience* (or, better still, persistence).

8.26–27   Even the most forward-looking Christians, however, need *aid* in their *weakness. We do not even know* (not *how* but) what *we ought to pray* for, *but through our inarticulate groans the Spirit himself is pleading* (not *for us*, but) in our stead. The difficulty nearest to Paul's mind becomes plain if we read on to verse 33 where the community is not on trial but is pleading for redress against their tormentors. Of course they will pray for an end to the hostility, but are their opponents to be disheartened, or ruined, or killed? Should they use the prayers of Jeremiah: 'Lord of Hosts, most righteous judge, testing the heart and mind, to you I have committed my cause; let me see your vengeance on them' (Jer. 11.20)? When Paul tells the community to 'persist in prayer', he adds 'Call down blessings on your persecutors – blessings, not curses' (12.12, 14). That calls for generosity of spirit; but even so, the blessings we want to bestow on our opponents may seem curses to them. At the end of the letter Paul says; 'Pray to God for me that I may be saved from unbelievers in Judaea' (15.30–31) – which would be gaining Paul's success by affronting his opponents or driving them from their convictions. Once you believe that prayers of petition and intercession can be effective, then the more earnest the prayer, the more perplexing the moral problem. Hence *inarticulate groans* from the community, and relying on the Spirit to plead *as God himself wills*. According to Mark 13.11 Jesus had given similar instruction to disciples who came under severe pressure.

8.28–30   But there are positive things to be said: *in everything, as we know, he co-operates for good with those who love God and are called according to his purpose.* In that REB0 translation, the 'he' who co-operates is presumably the Spirit, though perhaps 'God' is meant; but the old translation is still better: 'We know that all things work together for good for those who love God and are called according to his purpose' (as in NRSV). For fifty years that translation has been largely rejected because it has seemed patently untrue. But the variant translations are not much more acceptable, and it is better to ponder what Paul fairly certainly intended.

What he says about all things working together for good was a familiar thought in the ancient world. Even the apparently cynical writer of Ecclesiastes, already quoted on p. 73, can say that 'a sinner may do wrong and live to old age, yet I know that it will be well with those who fear God: their fear of him ensures this' (Eccles. 8.12). The Wisdom of ben Sirach remarks that 'the basic necessities of human life are water, fire, iron, salt, flour, honey, and milk, the juice of the grape, oil, and clothing – all these are good for the godfearing, but turn to evil for sinners' (Ecclus. 39.26–27 – about two hundred years before Romans). Paul hints at that over-optimistic belief but adds qualifications. The expected good is available to *those who love God* – a phrase very uncommon in Paul (he usually talks about God loving us) but standard in the Instruction, and meaning 'devotedly obedient'. It is there in the Ten Commandments ('I keep faith with thousands, those who love me and keep my commandments' (Ex. 20.6), and in the primary Jewish confession of faith ('Hear, Israel: the Lord is our God, the Lord is our one God; and you must love the Lord your God with all your heart', etc., (Deut. 6.4–5); repeated by Jesus in Mark 12.29–30, similarly in Matthew and Luke). Since Romans is much concerned with Christian responses to the Instruction, this Pauline reminder seems appropriate; but he makes a surprise move. For Paul, loving God means responding to the call to serve *his purpose*.

The *purpose* of God is a familiar but elusive Jewish theme. Psalm 33.10–11 says that 'The Lord frustrates the purposes of the nations; he foils the plans of the peoples. But the Lord's own purpose stands for ever, and the plans he has in mind endure for all generations.' At that level the Lord's purpose is to advance Israel and subdue the rest. Isaiah 46.10–13 begins more promisingly but reaches the same point: 'From the beginning I reveal the end, from ancient times what is yet to be; I say, "My purpose stands, I shall accomplish all that I please" … In Zion I shall grant deliverance for Israel my glory.' It is not surprising that a writer nearer, perhaps much nearer, Paul's time should say 'How can any human being learn what is God's plan? … Who ever came to know your purposes, unless you had given him wisdom and sent your holy spirit from heaven on high?' (Wisd. 9.13–17). Paul, however, is definite: God's purpose is that we should *share the likeness of his Son, so that he might be the eldest among a large family of brothers* – and from the whole thrust of the Epistle it is clear that he includes both Jews and non-Jews. In Paul's understanding of God the dominant features are wisdom and knowledge (11.33–36). Thus God knows beforehand what he will do and whom he will create, and in his wisdom does for them what is effective and what is loving. His purpose is to bring into being a social community that is like a family, that survives and is renewed on the model of God's Son who died and was raised from the dead. That role model is the only one available for the Christian community. It is *ordained* or *foreordained*. The old word is 'predestined' (as in NRSV) – which means that the destination is chosen, but not the names or the number of those who will reach it. The Greek word might be Englished as 'prehorizoned' – meaning that God has marked out the limits but not those who stray beyond them.

Those whom he foreordained, he also called. There is a summons to take up the benefits and responsibilities of God's family, a summons that does not simply arise from pressures within the family which come from outside. Those who respond are *justified* (welcomed as acceptable) and *glorified*. As it was said in 3.23 that 'all alike have sinned and are deprived of the divine glory', so now the new family of God is already touched with that glory – granted that 'we must share his sufferings if we are also to share his glory' (8.17).

8.31–39 *With all this in mind* (chapters 5–8 which begin and end with God's love) *what are we to say? If God is on our side* (which is the whole theme of 'justification', or acceptance by God) *who is against us? He did not spare his own Son* (as Abraham had been ready not to withhold his only son Isaac (Gen. 22.16) *but gave him up for us all; how can he fail to lavish every other gift upon us?* (5.9–10). *Who* among our opponents *will bring a* (damaging) *charge against those whom God has chosen? Not God, who* rightly accepts us (as members of his family, rather than *acquits*: these are not legal proceedings, but popular intimidation, as the following verses show). *Who will* denounce us (*pronounce judgment* is a stiff and formal translation)? *Not Christ, who died, or rather rose again; not Christ, who is at God's right hand* (the imagery, from Ps. 110.1, does not provide spatial information but indicates that Christ is in a position to tell God who are his) *and pleads our cause,* namely our need of help and support.

Father, Son, and Holy Spirit (v. 26) are on our side. *So what can separate us from* Christ's *love?* In the full flow of this triumphal rhetoric, there are listed the real dangers for Roman Christians, taken from Paul's missionary experiences (amply listed in II Cor. 6.4–5; 11.23–27; 12.10) and previously mentioned at 5.3. Not that this is something new and peculiar to Christians: Ps. 44.22 reminds us that God's people can expect not only hardship but also death. The world we live in is a dangerous place and its inhabitants are often corrupt and cruel. Having God on our side does not spare us from hardship, as it did not spare God's Son – *and yet, throughout it all, overwhelming victory is ours through him who loved us. I am convinced,* said Paul, *that there is nothing in death or life, in the realm of* (angelic) *spirits or superhuman powers* (if such there be), *in the world as it is or the world as it shall be, in the forces of the universe, in the heights* (of the planets most potent to harm) *or depths* (of the planets least able to help – if you believe in that kind of thing) – *nothing in all creation that can separate us from the love of God in Christ Jesus our Lord.*

On that high note – from which he will abruptly descend in 9.3 – Paul sums up his confidence in the gospel. Whether we live or die, whether our world is steadily the same or rapidly changing, whether we are helpless victims or ingenious exploiters of natural forces, whether we think ourselves surrounded by superhuman powers or determined by planetary influences – the one certainty is that we cannot be cut off from the powerful, mysterious love of God shown in the death and resurrection of Jesus Christ who is *our Lord* (see p. 48) – and our brother.

The redemption of Israel
9.1–5

It will be remembered that Paul's gospel was criticized because it was indifferent to sin, for relying on grace, not on obedience to the Instruction, and because he was hostile to God's Jewish people and destroyed God's credibility by allowing him to abandon the Jews (see p. 4). In chapters 1–8 Paul has dealt with the former criticism (the problem of Sin). Now, in chapters 9–11 he turns to the latter criticism – which becomes the problem of God.

In speaking of *my brothers, my kinsfolk by natural descent* (my relatives according to the flesh) he uses immense emphasis: *as a Christian enlightened by the Holy Spirit*, personally feeling *great grief and unceasing sorrow*. He touches on both Hellenistic moral conviction: *my conscience* and a Jewish rejection formula: *an outcast* (anathema), *cut off from Christ*. If it would help his fellow Jews he would deprive himself of the love of God in Christ Jesus (8.39).

He has no reservations about the outstanding, long-maintained privileges of the Jewish people. Despite long-standing disparagement of Jewish people and their religion, Christian readers should discern what those privileges are and show gratitude to the people who recorded them and suffered so much to preserve them. They are descendants of Israel and like Paul himself (11.1) proud of it. Israel was a fellowship of those who worship the true God and have been chosen by him to do so. In the stories told about their remote origins, Israel was the name given to the patriarch Jacob (Gen. 32.28; 35.10–12). Historically 'Israelite' referred to the religious tribal league described in Josh. 24. As a religious name it goes back at least a thousand years before Paul's time, more attractive to the people than the political term 'Jew'. Israelites were *chosen to be God's sons* ('Tell Pharaoh that these are the words of the Lord: Israel is my first-born son' (Ex. 4.22); 'When Israel was a youth, I loved him; out of Egypt I called my son' (Hos. 11.1)), *Theirs is the glory of the divine presence* ('The cloud covered the Tent of Meeting, and the glory of the Lord filled the Tabernacle' (Ex. 40.34); 'Holy, holy, holy is the Lord of Hosts; the whole earth is full of his glory' (Isa. 6.3)). *Theirs the covenants, the law, the temple worship* (with Abraham in Gen. 15 and

17, with Moses at Sinai in Ex. 19 onwards, and in Moab in Deut. 29–31; and so on) *and the promises* which are of special importance, as is shown by their repetition in Gen. 12.2–3, 7; 13.14–17; 17.4–8; 18.18; 22.16–18; 26.4; and 28.14. The promises are a package deal: Abraham is to be the originator not only of a great nation numerous beyond the possibility of counting but the father of a multitude of nations and kings. His empire will be so prosperous that it will become the standard of well-being for all other nations who will be judged according to their friendly or hostile attitude to Israel. Abraham's descendants will possess the land they occupy for ever, with encouragement to expand and possess the cities of their enemies. Not only so, but also *the patriarchs are theirs* (Abraham, Isaac, and Jacob), *and from them by natural descent came the Messiah*, God's anointed agent to rescue Israel from disaster.

To that we must return, but first there is a problem about the second part of verse 5 which in REB reads: *May God, supreme above all, be blessed for ever! Amen*. That is just the kind of ending that a Jew would use to bring a statement to a devout conclusion. But it is not the only, or even the most likely, rendering of Paul's Greek. NRSV prefers 'the Messiah, who is over all, God blessed for ever'. That, in a way without parallel in Paul, would assert that the Messiah is God. Our theological understanding of Christ does not rest upon the provoking conclusion of a Greek sentence; but it is worth while, at this point, to survey how he is regarded in Romans.

CHRISTOLOGY IN ROMANS

(1) There are 34 references to Christ, twice as many as any other designation. The most striking are in passages that speak of Christ's death and resurrection, e.g. 'Christ who died, or rather rose again … who is at God's right hand and pleads our cause' (8.34). And 'This is why Christ died and lived again, to establish his lordship over both dead and living' (14.9). So also 5.6–8; 6.4–5, 8–10; 8.11, 17, 34; 10.6–7; 14.15; 15.3. This is presumably the word of Christ (10.17) or the gospel of Christ (15.19–20) according to which Christ died and was raised by God. Hence the continuing activity of Christ is wholly dependent on the being and activity of God. There are examples in 5.8; 6.4; 8.11, 17; 14.18; 15.7 in which passages the activity of Christ is distinguished from the activity of God, in none of which is it possible to substitute 'God' for 'Christ'.

(2) Christ is often expanded to 'Christ Jesus' or 'Jesus Christ'. Once there is 'Christ Jesus our Lord' (6.23); then there is 'our Lord Jesus

Christ' (5.1; 15.6); 'the Lord Jesus Christ' (1.7; 13.14 – the latter according to the preferred Greek text, as in NRSV), and 'Jesus Christ our Lord' (1.4; 5.21; 7.25).

Since there are considerable variations in the ancient manuscripts, it is not possible to be certain about the distribution of these two phrases; but in general they are used differently and have different origins:

(*a*) Christ Jesus is the agent and means of God's activity: God judges through Christ Jesus (2.16); redemption, God's gift, life, and God's love are in Christ Jesus (3.24–5; 6.23; 8.2, 39). Further, Christ Jesus is the focus of Christian activity: slave, minister of Christ Jesus (1.1; 15.16); baptized into Christ Jesus (6.3); living in harmony (15.5); not condemned (8.1); alive to God (6.11); being proud (15.17).

(*b*) Jesus Christ, frequently joined with 'Lord', has strong connections with worship: 'Grace and peace to you from God our Father and the Lord Jesus Christ' (1.7 – see 15.6). The Lord Jesus Christ provides access to the divine call, grace, reconciliation, eternal life, and rescue from death (1.6; 5.1–2, 11, 21; 7.24–25). All this comes through the one man Jesus Christ (5.15, 17) – this is Last Adam language: proclaimed Son of God by an act of power that raised him from the dead … Jesus Christ our Lord (1.4). We ourselves have heard the call and belong to Jesus Christ (1.6); we put on the Lord Jesus Christ (13.14 as in NRSV).

(*c*) The word 'Lord' appears often in worship, but it begins in statements of belief: 'If the confession "Jesus is Lord" is on your lips, and the faith that God raised him from the dead is in your hearts, you will find salvation' (10.9). Similarly 4.24–5; 14.8–9.

(3) Jesus Christ our Lord is called Son of God in 1.3, 4, 9; 5.10; 8.3, 29, 32; and in 15.6 God is the Father of our Lord Jesus Christ.

That formal listing of Paul's practice shows that his christology – his way of thinking about Christ – put death and resurrection in the forefront, was responsive to divine and human activity, and included contributions from worship and creed. It includes a variety of designations, suitable for confessional and liturgical statements, again and again distinguishing Jesus from God but marking him as God's anointed agent and Son, disclosing him as the model of a new humanity.

Returning now to the question raised by verse 5, has not Paul done more than enough to place Jesus? What would he do more by calling him 'God' when (in the Hellenistic world) 'god' often conventionally indicated an outstanding person of exceptional piety, wisdom, or inspiration?

In fact, a robust assertion of God's supremacy is needed at this point, for what has happened to the promises? Israel's one-time expansive aims had failed, their territory was divided, they were a subject people enjoying (it is true) some security under Roman rule, but moving on the path that would taken them to revolt, national ruin, the end of Temple worship, and little evidence of 'the glory of the divine presence'.

The justification of God
9.6–11.32

9.6–13 *It cannot be that God's word has proved false.* Did not Isaiah say 'The grass may wither, the flower fade, but the word of our God will endure for ever' (Isa. 40.8). When Paul elsewhere speaks of 'God's word' he means the missionary proclamation, the Christian gospel. If God's promises to Israel have failed, perhaps the gospel – that God raised Christ from the dead – also fails, especially as Israel by and large has not accepted that gospel. The argument into which Paul now drives himself is a major rethinking of his Jewish relation to God. He is not playing with a side issue, as today's secularism may suppose, but giving a realistic appraisal to the perplexing uncertainties of human existence and to the unseen power that shapes it by his sole choice and will. It is worked out, in this part of the Epistle, in ways that apply to Jewish awareness, but the conclusions are equally important to Christians. When God gives his word, when he makes a promise, is he limiting his own freedom or is he defining a freedom that he now proceeds to explore? In 9.6–29 Paul considers what God is committed to in bestowing such benefits on Israel.

To understand the next stage of Paul's argument you need to know two famous stories, the first about Abraham who was married to Sarah. Despite the divine promise that Abraham would have innumerable descendants (Gen. 13.16), his wife had borne him no children. But Hagar, Sarah's slave-girl and Abraham's secondary wife was successful and produced a son, Ishmael (Gen. 16) who was the obvious inheritor of the divine promise. But despite Sarah's age, she too was promised a son and indeed gave birth to Isaac. Of him God said: 'Through Isaac's line your name will be perpetuated. I shall make a nation of the slave-girl's son, because he also is your child' (Gen. 21.12–13).

The other story is about Isaac's wife, Rebecca who was also child-less but conceived and was carrying twins in her womb. She sought guidance of the Lord and was told 'Two nations are in your womb, two peoples going their own ways from birth. One will be stronger than the other; the elder will be servant to the younger' (Gen.

25.21–23). Esau was born first, then Jacob; but Esau was caused to surrender to Jacob his right as the first-born.

These stories, nominally about founding fathers, are for practical purposes assessment stories about tribal groups – which is how Paul uses them. Small modifications of the fluent REB translation may indicate the background of his thought (9.6–8):

Not all the offspring of Israel are themselves *Israel.*
Nor is it true that all the children are Abraham's seed, but [quoting Gen. 21.12]
'in Isaac's line shall your seed be designated'.
That is to say, it is not simply *the children of*
Abraham's family *who are children of God*;
but *the children born through God's promise are*
treated *as Abraham's* children.

The old fashioned 'seed' (from AV) has been restored. Of course, 'descendants' is an entirely proper translation; but if you are talking of 'descendants' you are in the company of historians, genealogists, or probate lawyers – as REB supposes when it adds the word 'truly' in verse 7. But if the word 'seed' is retained for the Greek word 'sperm', you are thinking of farmers and gardeners. God is acting innovatingly, trying this seed rather than that seed, in the place where he intends to encourage growth and development. When God makes promises, he does not thereby destroy his sovereign freedom for innovation. He is certainly not entrapped by the traditional family system, or hampered by the rights of primogeniture, or forced to wait until he sees how Esau and Jacob will develop. In fact Esau turned out to be slow-witted and Jacob deceitful (Gen. 27). Paul goes even further and displays the divine freedom to act as God finds best by quoting *Jacob I love and Esau I hated*, the first oracle in Malachi. His remaining five oracles are savage condemnations of the descendants of Jacob. [*The purpose of God, which is a matter of his choice*, stands *firm*, *based not on human deeds but on the call of God.*]

9.14–18   That conviction prompts objections, and Paul allows a critic to speak in verses 14 and 19 – though each intervention allows him to press his conviction further. *Is God to be charged with injustice?* Impossible! That would run counter to the essence of Jewish devotion – as in the Song of Moses: 'Great is our God, the Creator, whose work is perfect, for all his ways are just, a faithful God who does no wrong; how righteous and true is he!' (Deut. 32.3–4). Paul, however, quoted a passage where God himself speaks (Ex. 33.13–23). Moses is

assured of God's favour and is known by name. He is promised that
the divine presence will go with him and the people as they journey.
But Moses requests more: 'Show me your glory.' God is willing to
display all his goodness, even to pronounce the most holy Name; but
'My face you cannot see, for no mortal may see me and live ... You
will see my back, but my face must not be seen.' In other words, you
cannot foresee what God will do; you can discover what he has done
only by hindsight. God reserves to himself his freedom to act: 'I shall
be gracious to whom I shall be gracious, and I shall have compassion
on whom I shall have compassion.' Indeed it is possible that the
most holy Name (Ex. 3.14) means 'I will be what I will be.'

The above quotation of Ex. 33.19 is the REB translation of the
Hebrew. Paul, however, in verse 15 quotes it from the Greek version
which is usually translated as REB has it: *I will show mercy ... and have
pity*. According to *The Concise Oxford Dictionary* mercy 'means
compassion or forbearance shown to enemies or offenders in one's
power', and that shifts the focus (in what Paul is saying here and in
11.30–32) a little in the wrong direction. Hence it would be better to
read verse 16 thus: [What happens in human affairs *does not depend
on human will or effort but on God's* unforced generosity – which is a
comforting reflection.]

Paul now takes an important step forward: God moves outside
Israel for an agent of his purpose, as is indicated in Ex. 9.16 (though
Paul modifies the wording). At that time the Israelites in Egypt were
a badly-treated, heavily exploited, captive foreign work-force,
engaged in building the storage cities of Pithom and Raamses. Not
surprisingly, they were regarded both as essential to the Egyptian
economy and a threat to it. At a time when Egypt was experiencing a
series of severe disasters, the Israelites (represented by an agitator
called Moses) demanded the right to withdraw their labour and go
about their own affairs. The Egyptian ruler Pharaoh took a strong
line and refused, again and again, to let them go. In Ex. 4–14 it is
said nine times that the Lord made Pharaoh obstinate. (The
familiar translation 'hardened Pharaoh's heart', as in NRSV, means
'strengthened his resolve'.) So (Paul explains) God's power is displayed and his fame is spread far beyond the Israelite community,
and spread by Pharaoh's agency. Not because Pharaoh is an
obedient or willing agent but precisely because he is stubborn and
unbelieving. *Thus he not only shows mercy* (or generosity) *as he chooses,
but also makes stubborn as he chooses*. He shows generosity to Pharaoh
by not destroying him, but allows Pharaoh's obstinacy to produce
an incompetent and disastrous military pursuit of the departing
Israelites. The stubbornness of Pharaoh is a classic example of a

ruler, convinced that his own judgment is right, being handed over to 'the wrath' (see p. 8). It is not God's arbitrary decision but an instance of what God has to do to control the interplay of human societies.

This particular illustration may well be remembered when Paul speaks of the hardening of Israel in 11.7, 25 and discusses the Christian's response to Roman authorities in chapter 13. Since, according to scripture, people are made in the image of God, it was natural for Jews, when speaking to God or about God, to use the conventions of ordinary speech. When Jews spoke theologically they presented God as a person of immense power and authority. But they were strictly forbidden to represent God by any kind of image or to misuse his name. Hence in telling stories about God they were aware that his nature and activity transcended all human activity – though sometimes they needed reminding: 'My thoughts are not your thoughts, nor are your ways my ways' (Isa. 55.8). Because Paul is drawing upon traditional stories he uses their anthropomorphic presentations of God's interaction with human beings, but what he says is not to be taken with naive literalism (so easily present to Western readers) but is to be transposed. Paul regarded the ruling principle of all things as 'wisdom and knowledge' (11.33) – that is, 'intelligence', in the widest meaning of that term and taking for granted that 'love' is an important sub-category of wisdom. It is instructive to discover what is said in Romans about God. In brief (*a*) The divine Intelligence is without rival, has no favourites, and is in two-way communication with human beings. (*b*) It is marked by truth and glory, has directing and controlling power, with the intention that what is right should be done for human beings, their societies, and the world they live in. (*c*) The supposed secrets of human intentions are known to the Intelligence which must discriminate and pass judgment with kindness or severity. If people persistently refuse what is right and reject the Intelligence's power to save, they will be overcome by their wrong choices and experience severity and anger. (*d*) But even wayward people, if they accept the power to save, will experience the Intelligence as forbearance, pity, mercy, kindness, faithfulness, and love.

The wise and knowing thing for the Egyptian administration to do might have been to make concessions to the Jewish labour force; but that prospect drove a vacillating tyrant into greater obstinacy, until he was first humiliated and then defeated.

9.19–21   Paul's critic speaks again in verse 19: *Why does God find fault, if nobody can resist his will* effectively? The simple answer would be that anybody can resist his will and thus cause God to find another way, perhaps more lengthy or disturbing, of carrying out his intention. That is why he finds fault. But Paul replies with a favourite Jewish illustration of the potter and his pottery. According to Gen. 2.7: 'The Lord God formed a human being from the dust of the ground and breathed into his nostrils the breath of life.' So God is like a potter, and some would say 'As clay is in the potter's hands to be moulded just as he chooses, so are human beings in the hands of their Maker to be dealt with as he decides' (Ecclus. 33.13). 'Out of the selfsame clay he fashions without distinction the pots that are to serve for clean uses and the opposite; and what the purpose of each one is to be, the moulder of the clay decides' (Wisd. 15.7, with references to Gen. 2 in 15.8 and 11). 'Will the pot contend with the potter, or the earthenware with the hand that shapes it? Will the clay ask the potter what he is making or his handiwork say to him, "You have no skill?"' (Isa. 45.9, rather stronger than Isa. 29.16 which Paul seems to be quoting here). The expected answer No! was strongly approved by the Hymn writer of the Dead Sea Scrolls, and often made by him: 'I have spoken in accordance with my knowledge, out of the righteousness given to a creature of clay. And how shall I speak unless Thou open my mouth; how understand unless Thou teach me?' (Thanksgiving Hymns XII.32 in Geza Vermes, *The Dead Sea Scrolls in English*, Penguin 1995, p.227). Not everyone gave the expected answer: unsurprisingly there is a hint of resistance in Job 10.8–9: 'Your hands shaped and fashioned me; and will you at once turn and destroy me? Recall that you have moulded me like clay; and would you reduce me to dust again?'

For the understanding of Romans, however, it is helpful to read Jer. 18.1–12. The prophet found the potter working at his wheel: 'Now and then a vessel he was making from the clay would be spoilt in his hands, and he would remould it into another vessel to his liking.' The application is to a nation or a kingdom which God may pull down and destroy or at any moment build or plant. Here the application is not to individuals but to communities, and that fits well Paul's present concern with the communities of Jews and Gentiles. The implication is that God can handle communities according to the changing needs of the larger situation and the varying responses of the particular communities – rather like the potter who makes one kind of pottery or another according to present need, or changes his intention when a lump of clay is resistant to his hand.

9.22–23   Can that illustration be taken further? Paul ventures on a possibility: 'Suppose God, instead of acting in an arbitrary manner (as you imagine) were to be acting thus'; but his tentative development in these two verses contains seven problems of interpretation. To mention only one of them: the word for *vessel* that was used in the pottery illustration appears again twice, but it was the common Greek word for 'thingummy' (hence in NRSV it is translated as 'object'). The old translation was 'vessels of wrath' and 'vessels of mercy' which will obviously not do; little better is REB 'tolerated vessels that were objects of retribution due for destruction' and 'vessels that were objects of mercy'. That wording makes the image clumsy. How can a pot be an object of retribution or mercy? Obviously an interpretation is needed that identifies the 'vessel' image in this argument, perhaps as follows:

> *But if it is indeed God's* intention
> *to display his* anger *and to make his power known,*
> *can it be that he has with great patience tolerated*
> communities that were agents of his anger
> designed to be destructive (or destructible),
> *precisely in order to make known the full wealth of his glory*
> on communities that are agents of his generosity,
> *prepared from the first* to display his *glory*?

For the substitution of 'anger' for *retribution*, see p. 7. This is not a speculative statement about individuals but about social groups and the functions they perform in God's historical dealings with mankind. At various times and places his sharp disapproval must be brought to bear and God tolerates the behaviour of certain communities because what they do is a necessary corrective. Their function is destructive. It is not discreditable to suppose that communities may do their work, have their day, and come to an end – in the providence of God. If the other possible translation 'destructible' were preferred, it would imply groups that displayed God's anger and then were destroyed by him. That would be grotesque. It would be almost equally misguided to imagine that God treats some with anger and rewards others with glory. As people involved in sinful social conditions, all people experience his anger, but from the beginning are predestined to display his glory. Paul, strongly aware of the dark side of God's working, yet ends triumphantly with God's generosity and glory.

It is instructive to observe the extent of Paul's awareness in history and location. He relies on a God who interacted with Abraham, Isaac, and Jacob, and with Moses and Pharaoh; who spoke through Elijah and Isaiah; who demonstrated sovereignty through David;

and in most recent days proclaimed his Son by an act of power that raised him from the dead. Paul's mind moved easily from Judaea and Jerusalem as far round as Illyricum, taking in Asia Minor and Achaia, reaching Rome and planning to visit Spain. He was deeply concerned with bringing together Jews and Gentiles, though firmly maintaining his own Israelite status 'of the stock of Abraham, of the tribe of Benjamin' (11.1). As a Jew he knew that God was in some way at work in the twists and turns of history, and was convinced that God had set in motion a wholly new phase of social existence (see p. 14. As a Hellenistic Jew of the Roman world he was strongly persuaded that social life needed firm direction, orderliness, and justice. Hence his treatment of governmental authority in chapter 13. But if God was in some way at work, how account for the dreadful and disastrous episodes? Hence Paul's doctrine of the divine anger, of the divine toleration of 'agents of his anger' – which are perhaps to be used and then come to an end. In 13.4 the governing authorities are 'God's agents of punishment bringing retribution ("anger") on the offender' – at present to be used, but then what? The argument is not easy, and might begin to imply that God should do evil that good might come of it. But if God is indeed related, directly or indirectly, to the historical course of peoples and their history, then this is an area of discussion where questions are asked and answers must be attempted. Paul's tentative exploration may not solve the problem but it may provide the theological context in which it must be discussed.

9.24–26   Chapter 9 began with deep sorrow for Paul's Jewish kins-folk who had not accepted God's action in Christ Jesus. But God shows generosity where he chooses: those *whom he has called* are *from Jews and Gentiles alike*. Once again (as earlier in the Epistle: 1.5, 13 and 3.29) Paul is a Jew who brings non-Jews within the orbit of God's goodness. He supports his position and commends it by a bold use of Hosea's words – hearing which a Gentile Christian might suppose that the prophet had long ago extended God's welcome to non-Jews. But Jewish Christians would presumably know that Hosea had been making a promise to Israel (pictured as an unfaithful wife penitently returning to her husband) – in fact northern Israel, at that time unpitied by God, unforgiven, ruined by war, and dispersed. Paul describes what God has done for Gentiles in words that belonged to God's promise for a repentant Israel. That has two consequences: it indicates the depth of the divine generosity; and it permits the hope that if God does this for hostile Gentiles, how much more will he surely do for unresponsive Israel!

9.27–29   Yet the present position of the majority of Jews, in Paul's mind, was not encouraging. Hosea's words which he had just quoted were preceded by the famous promise to Abraham that the Israelites would be as countless as the sands of the sea; and that reminded Paul how Isa. 10.22–23 had dealt with the same promise: *only a remnant shall be saved, for the Lord's sentence on the land will be summary and final.* Cutting down the promise of huge abundance to a mere remnant sounds hopeless and despairing, but it is at least something, perhaps even the beginning of something. So for example according to the prophet Micah, the Lord once said 'I shall restore the lost as a remnant and turn the outcasts into a mighty nation' (Micah 4.7 – in 5.7–9 indeed the remnant becomes aggressively dominant). Paul, however, is content with Isaiah's rueful comment: *If the Lord of Hosts had not left us* seed (see p. 83) *we should have become like Sodom, and no better than Gomorrah* (Isa. 1.9).

The Bible has a good many references to Sodom and Gomorrah which were ancient rift valley communities somewhere in the region of the Dead Sea. Among nomadic tribes, they had a (probably deserved) reputation for gross immorality (see Gen. 18.16–19.29). It is commonly assumed that Sodom's wickedness was sodomy, but Isa. 1.10–16 links them with injustice, indifference to the oppressed, the fatherless, and widows – and Paul actually quotes Isa. 1.9 in verse 29. Most references to Sodom and Gomorrah indicate total destruction. But if Paul was rightly hopeful, God would not destroy his Jewish people but would leave them seed, a living centre where their unique awareness of God would contribute to the world's Gentile life.

9.30–33   If in 9.6–29 Paul considers what God is committed to in bestowing his benefits on Israel, he now turns to what Jews and Gentiles are committed to in accepting these benefits. In 9.30–10.10 he restates his argument in terms of 'righteousness', in 10.4–17 in terms of *faith*. In 9.30 there are Gentiles *who made no effort after righteousness*, but in 10.20 God revealed himself to those who were not looking for him. In 9.31 it is admitted that Israel *made great efforts after a law of righteousness*, but in 10.21 they are *a disobedient and defiant people*. Hence a complex but carefully constructed section, intended to stick in the memory of hearers and readers.

But what does *righteousness* mean as it is used here? If *righteousness* (no longer a very useful English word) means the condition of being morally right, how can Paul say that Gentiles *made no effort after righteousness*? Paul may have read nothing by his contemporary Roman Stoic moralist Seneca, but (to judge by his own use of popular ethical teaching, e.g. 'conscience' in 2.15; 9.1; 13.5), he cannot have been ignorant of Stoic earnestness. He himself said that there are Gentiles who, not possessing the law, carry out its precepts and are subject to conscience (2.14–15). What then is this *righteousness* that failed to arouse Gentile eagerness. Earlier in the Epistle, God's righteousness is described as his saving goodness; our righteousness as our acceptability to God (pp. 5 and 27). Here something more comprehensive is required; righteousness is a social existence under the direction, protection, and correction of the God known in the tradition of Israel. That righteousness the Gentiles did not pursue, but came upon it by faith. That is to say, they placed their reliance on him who raised Jesus from the dead (1.3–4, and see p. 23) and discovered the rightness of it for their community life.

Yet *Israel made great efforts after a law of righteousness, but never attained to it*. That presumably means – 'presumably' because the sentence is sparsely written – that the Jews in general gave strict adherence to the Mosaic law in order to strengthen the bonds of the community directed, protected, and corrected by God. *But never attained to it*. Paul's criticism of his own people has already been expressed in 2.21–29. The history of the Jewish people for two hundred years before Paul's day shows the penetration of Greek life-style, the religious discontent of such groups as the Qumran community, the removal of Jewish rulers and their replacement by the Romans who countenanced the dominance of an immensely rich Temple hierarchy, and tension between Judaea and conservative, rural Galilee. These disorders were no doubt the result of errors and mischief at all levels, but they were not divine punishment for neglect of Mosaic laws. Nor would a radical programme of law-abiding *deeds* remove the disorders and ensure survival and renewal. The only way to survive in a corrupt and disordered world is by *faith*. Israel's *efforts were not based on faith but, mistakenly, on deeds*. We now know that the community of Qumran was worried, as Paul was, about the state of Israel. They regarded the Council of the sect as 'the elect of Goodwill who shall atone for the land and pay to the wicked their reward. It shall be that tried wall, that precious cornerstone, whose foundations shall neither rock nor sway in their place' (*Community Rule* VIII.6–8). The sectarians were presenting themselves as the absolutely reliable and indestructible foundation of a renewed Israel. The precious corner-stone, an image taken from Isa. 28.16, is the symbolic beginning of a new sanctuary. Anyone who puts confidence in it will not be humiliated. Paul also uses that imagery from Isa. 28, but he adds more stone imagery from Isa. 8.13–14. There it is the Lord himself who 'will become a sanctuary, a stone one strikes against; for both houses of Israel he will become a rock one stumbles over – a trap and a snare for the inhabitants of Jerusalem'. For the Qumran sect, their radical new beginning was an even stricter observance of the Mosaic Instruction. For Isaiah it was the Lord himself and for Paul it was the Lord's special representative, Jesus Christ – even though official Israel had taken offence against him. *But he who has faith in it* (the identification of Jesus as the corner-stone) *will not be put to shame*. A modern reader may be perplexed by this use of imagery if he supposes that Paul is intending to prove something from scripture. But it should be remembered that Paul is thinking about Jews and addressing them. The flexible use of imagery in scripture permits, even encourages the devout mind to move in this and that direction. Paul uses the immovable stone – an obvious image of what is certain in religion – and points to what may be built upon it and to hostility that may be expected.

10.1–4 At this point Paul begins to reflect on the *salvation* of his Jewish kinsmen. Not simply individual Jews like himself who would be accounted for by 'only a remnant shall be saved' in 9.27; but the Jewish people as a community dear to God. It was explained on p. 5 that *salvation* means the rescue of a community from its degradation ('saved from the anger' 5.9) and the disclosure of unseen possibilities ('saved by his life' 5.10; 'with this hope we were saved' 8.24). The conditions for salvation will be stated in 10.9 and 13; and in 11.14 and 26 he will still be worrying whether some or all of Israel will be saved. But here he testifies *to their zeal for God*. That he has already admitted in 2.17–20: their zeal to proclaim, demonstrate, and spread the knowledge of God. He himself had outstripped most of his Jewish contemporaries by his boundless devotion to the traditions of his ancestors. He had savagely persecuted the church of God and tried to destroy it (Gal. 1.13–14) – what he admits was his 'zeal for religion' (Phil. 3.6). He was not the only one. The Qumran group laid down 'rules of conduct for the Master in those times with respect to his loving and hating. Everlasting hatred in a spirit of secrecy for the men of perdition! ... He shall be a man zealous for the Precept whose time is for the Day of Revenge' (*Community Rule* IQS IX.21–23). That kind of thing can become fanatical, not merely *ill-informed* (as appears today in some fundamentalist kinds of religion). Paul's fellow-Jews were not properly aware of the results that their zeal was having. *They ignore* (he says) *God's way of righteousness* – or perhaps think they are maintaining it as they *try to set up their own*. Think back to the meaning of 'righteousness' in this argument: a social existence under the direction, protection, and correction of God. Jewish zeal has changed that to 'under the direction, protection, and correction of its Jewish defenders'. For that reason the defenders are shutting themselves out from the other two meanings of righteousness: the saving goodness of God and their acceptability to him.

But *Christ is the end of the law and brings righteousness for everyone who has faith*. The word *end*, like Paul's corresponding Greek word, has many meanings. Here there is an important double meaning: purpose and termination. Christ fulfils the purpose for which the law was given and so brings it to its proper conclusion. It goes without saying that Paul was not abandoning the scriptures. He was leaving them as law and returning to them as instruction, as he says in 15.4: 'The scriptures written long ago were all written for our instruction.' The further discussion of Israel's salvation draws abundantly on scripture; and the treatment of Christian morality in chapter 13 is firmly attached to the Commandments. But scripture is no longer the source from which a restricted group of people takes the symbolic rituals which define and preserve its identity. In 2.25–29 and 4.9–12 circumcision and uncircumcision are in their way important, but neither is requisite for membership of the people of God. Neither the obligation of these rituals nor the performance of them gains, or guarantees, or preserves acceptability with God. Only faith in God whose saving activity is displayed in the death and resurrection of Christ – which perhaps like 'a stone to trip over, a rock to stumble against' lies hidden in scripture; but anyone 'who has faith in it will not be put to shame' (9.33).

10.5–13   Paul does not regard Jewish misplaced zeal as a late perversion: it goes right back to Moses himself. According to what was said in Lev. 18.1–5 Israel was to keep God's laws and conform faithfully to his statutes so as to distinguish them from the customs of the Egyptians whom they were leaving and the customs of Canaan where they were arriving. Whoever keeps God's laws and statutes will have life through them. But Paul finds another strain in the Instruction that is more congenial to *righteousness that comes by faith*. For a while his mind turns to Moses' second oration in Deut. 5–11 as he prepares the people to enter the land where they are to defeat and exterminate the native inhabitants, refuse marriage with them, and destroy their sacred images (Deut. 7.1–6). They must not say to themselves 'My own strength and energy have gained me this wealth', nor 'It is because of my righteousness that the Lord has brought me in to occupy this land' (Deut. 8.17; 9.4).

Those modest indicators would indeed be agreeable to Paul's

insistence on acceptability to God by faith, but how can they prevail against the great bulk of Mosaic laws and statutes with their imperious, ever-present demands? Paul found his answer where some of his contemporaries also looked: almost at the end of Moses' great oration, just before the dramatic choice between life-and-good or death-and-evil. It sounds the very opposite of fanatical religion.

> This commandment that I lay on you today
> is not too difficult for you or beyond your reach.
> It is not in the heavens, that you should say,
> 'Who will *go up to the heavens* for us
> to fetch it and tell it to us,
> so that we can keep it?'
> Nor is it beyond the sea, that you should say,
> 'Who *will cross the sea* for us
> to fetch it and tell it to us,
> so that we can keep it?'
> It is a *thing very near to you*,
> *on your lips and in your heart*
> ready to be kept (Deut. 30.11–14).

It implies that the Instruction is not mysterious rules known only to the heavenly world but is part of the every-day awareness of Israel; it does not need to be sought outside Israel's borders but is the common custom of their land. These words were a much-favoured quotation of Paul's slightly older contemporary, the Alexandrian philosopher Philo. In his writings religious moralism is temptingly held out as an alternative to religious fanaticism, though both fail to see the 'good news' that Paul is presenting. One example of Philo will suffice.

> Having learnt how great an evil is the wrath of God, and how great a good is the gladness of God, stir not up to thine own destruction aught that deserves His anger, but practise those things only by which thou shalt make God glad. And these thou shalt not find by traversing long roads where no foot has trodden, or by crossing the seas where no ship has sailed, nor by pressing without a pause to the boundaries of land or ocean. For they do not dwell apart in the far distance, nor are they banished from the habitable world, but, as Moses says, the good is stationed just beside thee and shares thy nature, close bound with the three most essential parts, heart, mouth, and hands, since to think and speak and do the morally good is the essential thing, a fullness

composed of good purposing, good action, and good speaking (*On Dreams* II.179–80: Loeb Library, Philo V).

Philo said that kind of thing so many times that he presumably thought it worth saying; but it wholly misses the moral need of particular people under stress and suggests no way of handling social morality. It has not begun to understand what Paul means by a society enslaved by Sin – as in chapter 6. Paul has in mind the hard-pressed person who says in effect: 'Would that we could reach up into heaven and persuade a saviour to come down. Would that a saviour might reach down and find us in the abyss of despair!' Paul's words in fact recall the seaman's peril in Ps. 107.26. Thus, as the Mosaic Instruction nears its climax in Deut. 30, Paul finds a discounting of human effort (climbing the heavens, crossing the sea) in order to please and placate God, and its replacement by recognition and acceptance of what is near at hand. He constructs a simple, easily-memorable formula for a Jew who enters the Christian community:

> *If the confession 'Jesus is Lord' is on your lips,*
> *and the faith that God raised him from the dead*
> *is in your heart, you will find salvation.*
> *For faith in the heart leads to righteousness,*
> *and confession on the lips leads to salvation.*

Paul's fellow-Jews would understand what his words mean, but we need to remind ourselves of what lies behind them. 'Righteousness' was described on p. 90, and 'salvation' on p. 5. Suggestions for a modern understanding of 'Lord' were made on p. 48. 'Heart' means your will or motive force, and confessing with the lips implies a public statement of convictions. Faith that God raised Jesus from the dead is therefore something more than a sturdy belief that the Gospel resurrection stories are factually true. Rather than that, it is confidence that God can bring new life out of dismaying failure, can lead the believer to discover what is right in the emerging situation of hitherto unseen possibilities.

This, however, applies not only to Jews but to everybody, as *scripture says*. Isa. 28.16, previously quoted at 9.33, implies no restriction: therefore *No one who has faith in him will be put to shame.* That is, no embarrassing rejection, no disillusionment, *No distinction between Jew and Greek, because the same Lord is Lord of all.* As the prophet Joel said *Everyone who calls on the name of the Lord will be saved* (Joel 2.32). 'Name' means reputation: if you call on God who is well-known to love his people and rescue them in need, you will be saved. It is appropriate to take note of the situation for which Joel made that promise: God would pour out his spirit on all mankind, there would be a remnant as the Lord had promised, and all the nations would be brought to judgment. The prophecy is less than coherent but it provided indications in scripture that the destinies of Jews and Gentiles were inter-related.

10.14–21   Nor was it true that Israel responded to the Lord's instructions whereas the Gentiles did not. An appeal to God, such as Joel suggested, depended on hearing about him. Hearing is possible if someone spreads the news, and how could they do that unless they were sent? Hence the bringer of good news is rooted in scripture, as in Isa. 52.7 'How beautiful on the mountains are the feet of the herald, the bringer of good news, announcing deliverance' (used again in Nahum 1.15 – the conviction that is expressed in 'the gospel of God' in Rom. 1.1, 9, 16). Such news should prompt acceptance but *not all have responded*. Isaiah's exultant promise is strengthened by the conviction that 'the whole world from end to end shall see the deliverance wrought by our God' because his servant (Israel) 'will achieve success, he will be raised to honour, high and exalted'. But alas! 'Many nations recoil at the sight of him, and kings curl their lips in disgust' (Isa. 52.10–15). *As Isaiah says, who believed when they heard us?* The implication of that (which will shortly become plain) is that Jews are now withholding response to the good news which Gentiles are welcoming. *So then faith does come from hearing,* and the word that is near to you (of v. 8) is *the word of Christ* i.e. the good news contained in the death and resurrection of Christ as announced by the apostolic messengers.

Paul now brings this part of his argument to an end with two rhetorical questions that look perplexing on the printed page but can be uttered effectively by an experienced speaker. (*a*) *Can it be that they never heard?* with stress on *heard* – perhaps because God intended only a limited circulation? Of course not! Remember Ps. 19 which begins with the universal message of God's creation, continues with the perfection of his law, and ends with personal acceptability to the Lord. (*b*) *Can it be that Israel never understood?* with stress on *Israel* (not on *understood*, which might be better translated 'made no acknowledgment'). Is it credible that the Lord's own people, long experienced in the blessings of Ps. 19, could fail to acknowledge *the word of Christ* which Gentiles were accepting? Alas! it was all too likely as Moses had foreseen (Deut. 32.21) and as Isaiah had daringly spoken. Others would be more responsive than the Lord's own people.

In the end what we are committed to by accepting God's benefits is faith and the universality of faith. To repudiate either is to be disobedient and hostile. On that showing the Jews appear as *a disobedient and defiant people*.

11.1–6 Then *has God rejected his people*? Rejected them as what? Has God pushed them aside (that is what the verb implies) as people to be helped or as agents of his purpose? It is often said in scripture that God intends to reject them or has indeed done so. For example: 'I shall cast off what is left of my people, my own possession, and hand them over to their enemies. They will be plundered, a prey to all their enemies' (II Kings 21.14: they are not to be helped); and 'I shall reject this city of Jerusalem which once I chose, and the house where I promised that my name should be' (II Kings 23.27: they are no longer to represent the name and reputation of God). The Psalmist often complains that they have been rejected: 'You have rejected and humbled us and no longer lead our armies to battle ... You have exposed us to the contempt of our neighbours, to the gibes and mockery of those about us' (Ps. 44.9, 13 – the whole psalm is worth reading, for Israel's survival and God's reputation are at stake).

But to Paul that is unthinkable. Who knows better than Paul who is a genuine Israelite, a former opponent of God, but chosen by grace to be apostle of the Gentiles? And scripture is not wholly disheartening. The Psalmist's voice is sometimes encouraging: *God has not rejected the people he acknowledged of old as his own* (Ps. 94.14 – though Paul confidently changes the psalmist's promise: 'the Lord will not abandon' to his own *has not rejected*). The NRSV translation has 'whom he foreknew', the verb already used at 8.29. It means to appoint beforehand to a position or function, like Israel who was formed in the womb to be the servant of the Lord (Isa. 49.1, 5). And Paul has already said that 'the Jews were entrusted with the oracles of God' and other numerous and high privileges (3.2; 9.4–5). The prophet Samuel reassured the Israelites when they repented of their wickedness: 'For his great name's sake the Lord will not cast you off, because he has resolved to make you his own people' (I Sam. 12.22).

Perhaps God might do that by exploiting the reliability of a remnant – of which there was certainly one famous example. When (some nine hundred years before Paul) the prophet Elijah was in conflict with king Ahab and his paganizing queen Jezebel, the prophet believed himself to be the one remaining devotee of the covenant God of Israel. But it was disclosed to him that God could put seven thousand supporters at his disposal. The story is told in I Kings 19 and Elijah is firmly put in his place by a nice expression of the divine pleasure: *I have left myself seven thousand* (Paul again changes 'I shall leave' to *I have left*). Elijah may have let the situation get out of hand, but God had not. The outcome was determined not first and last by the notable deeds of Elijah but by the divine choice and grace. Of course what Elijah did was of outstanding importance, but without supportive and directive grace there would be no end result. Paul himself was not chosen for his merits or devotion to God, if one looks back at his own previous history (p. 91). If it perhaps seems odd that Paul should be so anxious about the salvation of Israel, so (it should be remembered) were his contemporaries at Qumran. The leader and members of the sect thought they had a representative responsibility to atone for Israel, and that they attempted by strict obedience to the Mosaic Instruction and to the additional rules by which they guarded it. Paul, however, urged faith upon his readers, otherwise *grace would cease to be grace*.

11.7–10 All the same, faith does not come easily if *Israel has not attained what Israel sought*, (see 9.31 and p. 90) if only *the chosen few have attained it. The rest were hardened*: like Pharaoh in 9.17–18 their resolve was strengthened to do what they pleased (p. 84), strengthened by God himself. Long ago Moses complained that the Israelites had seen what God did to Pharaoh, with great signs and portents; but God had not given them the ability to understand (Deut. 29.2–4). To pick up a bitter phrase from Isa. 29.10 'the Lord had given them a spirit of stupefaction'. Paul was not alone in his unhappiness about the Jewish people. 'This people's wits are dulled; they have stopped their ears and shut their eyes, so that they may not see with their eyes, nor listen with their ears, nor understand with their wits, and then turn and be healed' (Isa. 6.10 – the whole chapter should be read, including the despairing conclusion that the great tree would be felled and only a stump remain). This hardening, this strengthening of a resolve to behave wrongly is a clear example of being handed over to the Anger (p. 8). To put it more plainly: if a group of people persevere in doing what is wrong and what they know to be wrong, they cannot expect to be shielded from unpleasant consequences but must bear them to the full. So much so that Paul now transfers to hostile Jews curses that the Psalmist applied to his enemies.

Two psalms come to mind (35 and 69), both expressing acute misery. In Ps. 35.7–8 the enemies without provocation have spread a net to catch the Psalmist and have dug a pit to trap him – may they be caught in their own net, may they fall into their own pit and be destroyed. Psalm 69 was drawn upon and quoted by the Evangelists to mark the sufferings of Jesus, especially the offering of vinegar: 'When I was thirsty they gave me vinegar to drink' (Ps. 69.21). The psalmist's misery turns into anger against his enemies, and Paul appropriates some of his curses for (as he sees it) the enemies of God – such as he himself had once been (5.10). What the quotation in verse 9 implies, however, is not clear. Perhaps it is simply a good all-purpose curse; but perhaps *their table* in verse 9 refers to strict Pharisaic eating rules, forbidding a common table for Jews and Gentiles. Problems of that kind are dealt with in chapter 14.

11.11–16 What now follows looks like making the best of a bad job. But consider how Paul is placed. He is addressing a community of Christians, some of whom are Jews (to judge from the detailed reference to Jewish history and scripture), many, however, are Gentiles. They have accepted the lordship of a Jewish activist who, within recent memory had been crucified by the Gentile administration of a Jewish country. His lordship demanded faith in his death and resurrection, but not Pharisaic devotion to the Mosaic Instruction, and certainly not Gentile devotion to the many gods and lords of ancient piety. This was a major shift in the self-awareness of people in the Mediterranean world. It was surely God's doing, but what an odd way of doing it! *Through a false step* on the part of Israel *salvation has come to the Gentiles*. As Paul has already said Jews regarded themselves as 'a light to those in darkness' (2.19) – and indeed with the encouragement of Isaiah: 'I have formed you, and destined you to be a light for peoples, a lamp for nations' (Isa. 42.6); 'This people I have formed for myself, and they will proclaim my praises' (Isa. 43.21); 'I have formed you, and destined you to be a light for peoples, restoring the land and allotting once more its desolate holdings' (Isa. 49.8); 'You will be called priests of the Lord and be named ministers of our God. You will enjoy the wealth of nations and succeed to their riches' (Isa. 61.6).

Paul is convinced that though Israel had stumbled their fall was not final. For assessing the present untoward situation he makes four more or less tentative proposals.

(a) Since *salvation has come to the Gentiles*, this will stir the Jews to envy (v. 11) – relying on the unique suggestion in Deut. 32.21 already quoted in 10.19. *As an apostle to the Gentiles* Paul presses hard, *in the hope of stirring those of* his *own race to envy, and so saving some of them* (vv. 13–14). That modest aim suggests that he was aware of the criticism (and sensitive to it) that he should be evangelizing the Jews, not the Gentiles. What it is that Jews might envy is not obvious. If Paul was right in thinking that a major shift in social self-awareness was taking place, then by accepting the gospel Gentiles were better placed than Jews to take advantage of it. Jews had long been taught that Jerusalem would become the acknowledged world-centre. For example: 'Many nations will go, saying "Let us go up to the mountain of the Lord, to the house of Jacob's God, that he may teach us his ways and we may walk in his paths". For instruction issues from Zion, the word of the Lord from Jerusalem' (Micah 4.2; see also Isa. 2.1–5; 25.6–9). But now the world-centre, even in imagination, was moving away from Jerusalem, perhaps to Rome.

(*b*) If their false step means the enrichment of the world (i.e. society generally), if their falling short ('defeat' is a possible translation) means the enrichment of the Gentiles, how much more will their coming to full strength mean! (v. 12). An optimistic argument (much used by Jewish teachers) from less to greater. Presumably it is hoped that Israel will accept the gospel, not by individual conversions, but as a community.

(*c*) Since *their rejection* (of the gospel) *has meant the reconciliation of the world* (i.e. Hellenistic society) to God (i.e. believers are no longer at enmity with God, as in 5.10) *their acceptance* of the gospel will mean *nothing less than life from the dead* (v. 15). Based on the death and resurrection of Jesus, the gospel asserts that God can take a hopeless, ruined situation and produce a new, unforeseen quality of life.

(*d*) Verse 16 seems to rely on the contagious quality of holiness. *The first loaf* refers to the command of Num. 15.17–21 that when bread is baked the first loaf is given to the priests, so that the family can eat the rest of the batch with God's blessing. *The root* and *the branches* are more difficult to discover. Perhaps Isa. 37.31–32 suggests the image: 'The survivors left in Judah will strike fresh root below ground and yield fruit above ground, for a remnant will come out of Jerusalem.' And the people of Qumran used the image of the sacred tree: 'The bud of the shoot of holiness of the Plant of truth was hidden and not esteemed; and being unperceived, its mystery was sealed' (IQH VIII.10). Is Paul trying to persuade himself that the remnant composed of Jewish Christians will take root again and promote vigorous growth – which becomes a symbol of the restoration of Israel? Or by *the first loaf* does he imply the patriarchs, Abraham and the other forefathers of Israel – who are mentioned in verses 28–29. At this point he cannot find a really suitable image or persuasive argument, nor can he surrender himself to the thought that the majority of Israel have abandoned and been abandoned.

11.17–24   Having thus pleaded the cause of Israel that is absent, Paul now defends Jewish Christians that are present against Gentile superiority. He imagines a well-rooted cultivated olive tree (which represents the social and religious culture of Israel), from which some (unproductive) branches have been cut off (the majority of Jews, alas!). Cuttings from wild olives have been grafted in, a standard procedure for improving production according to Columella, an authoritative writer on Roman agriculture, contemporary with Paul (representing Gentile converts). Thus Paul implies that the accession of Gentile converts will invigorate the basic religious tradition. That is not *against nature* (as v. 24 is unfortunately translated) but it is not in the course of nature: the cultivator has done his pruning and grafting. This olive imagery perhaps comes from Jer. 11.16–17 where Israel was once 'an olive tree, leafy and fair' but set on fire, and its branches consumed. Paul's imagery is less drastic, but it becomes less plausible. Jewish branches were cut off for lack of faith, Gentile grafts will be cut off if their faith is replaced by pride, and it is within God's power to graft the pruned Jewish branches back – *if they do not continue faithless*. Obviously the olive imagery is now restricting what Paul needs to say, and it is worth asking why he used it at all. He intended to say that God's people needed renewal of life. Drastic action was needed, in the human sense, as drastic as pruning and grafting in olive production. God has to show *severity* in order to act with *kindness*, to which of course people respond with hostility or overconfidence. But the only required response, from whichever party, is faith.

11.25–32 Now at last Paul discloses his prophetic-cum-apostolic insight: *there is a divine secret* to share with his readers. NRSV retains the old translation 'mystery', a technical term in some of the private religions of the ancient world, referring to their secret teachings and rituals. Paul's use is different. Secrecy is discarded, and perplexity is relieved when the Spirit discloses to 'stewards of the mysteries of God' (I Cor. 4.1) the divine wisdom at work in the divine purposes. For Paul there was no 'simple gospel'. Why had earthly powers crucified the Lord of glory (I Cor. 2.6–10)? What will happen to those still alive when the great transformation takes place (I Cor. 15.51–54)? What is holding back the transformation (II Thess. 2.7)? And here in Romans, 'What will happen to Israel?' In chapters 9–11, Paul has related the process by which he arrived at the 'mystery' and tells them the result *to keep you from thinking yourselves wise* enough to work it out without apostolic aid.

In verse 7 he said that only the chosen few attained what Israel sought; the rest were hardened. Now in verse 25 he discloses that *this partial hardening has come on Israel only until the Gentiles have been admitted in full strength.* His meaning would be better grasped with a simpler rendering of his Greek: 'until the fullness of the Gentiles has entered in'. 'Entered in' recalls the well-known Gospel sayings about entering into the kingdom, life, and joy and in John 10.9 into the fold, suggesting that Paul is drawing on words that go back to the Jesus tradition. The admission of Gentiles *in full strength* presumably indicates a hope that a major adhesion of Gentiles and Gentile communities would take place, sufficient to prompt Jewish communities to think again and take their proper place in the church.

Once that has happened, the whole of Israel (as a community, rather than all individual Jews) *will be saved.* Its rejection will be reversed and its former role restored, though in a new and unexpected fashion. This 'mystery' gives meaning to half-understood hopes in scripture: Ps. 14 (already quoted in 3.10–11) ends by saying; 'If only deliverance for Israel might come from Zion! (see Paul's previous reference to Zion in 9.33). When the Lord restores his people's fortunes, let Jacob rejoice, let Israel be glad'. Isaiah 59.20–21 imagines a *deliverer* coming to Zion (in the Greek coming for the sake of Zion, in Paul's quotation coming *from Zion*) to *remove wickedness from Jacob,* so that the Lord grants them a covenant (defined in the words of Isa. 27.9) *when I take away their sins.*

With those quotations in mind some thought must be given to Paul's reliance on scripture, especially as he makes four times as many reference per page in chapters 9–11 when compared with the rest of the Epistle. Consequently the commentary on these chapters is obliged to identify, interpret, and explain the force of quotations again and again. We are trying to follow the thought of a writer who knew a great deal of scripture by heart, knew it in Hebrew and Greek, pondered over it, and made connections that were not at first obvious. He was not going to scripture for 'proof' of doctrine or for 'unbreakable rules' of behaviour when he said that God's word cannot prove false (9.6). For him scripture contained knowledge of the nature and freedom of God, of his government of the world, and of the ambiguous responses of human beings, Jewish and Gentile. Paul therefore was prompted to revise his understanding of scripture and to pick up new indications when major changes were taking place in human affairs.

One more comment is necessary. In the Epistle Paul uses the word Sin forty-five times in the singular, only three times in the plural (4.7; 7.5; 11.27, all with Old Testament reference). His remarkable use of the singular was explained on pp. 20–21. When in this chapter he expects the Deliverer to *remove wickedness* and *take away their sins* he intends more than forgiveness, even than atonement. He thinks that

God will deter their sinning, making them a new people with a different outlook on human life. It is worth looking at the 'brand snatched from the fire' in Zech. 3.2–5.

God's essential intention, never broken, is *to show mercy to all mankind. The gracious gifts of God and his calling* (to share and enjoy them with other people) *are irrevocable. The patriarchs*, like Abraham in chapter 4, were called to father many nations, to disclose the pattern of life in this world under the divine lordship. But the world is a difficult and dangerous place. Social groups driven by fear and resentment, by advantage and disadvantage, become adversaries rather than associates – hence the *shutting* of *all mankind in the prison* of *their disobedience*. In this condition of co-operative hostility the presence of however good a law merely strengthens, even sanctions, the enmity. Hence the divine lordship devises a strange, unexpected intervention to restore the rightful heritage of mankind: putting death and resurrection in the forefront and receiving the allegiance of Gentiles before the faithful response of Israel.

> *Just as formerly you* (Gentiles) *were disobedient to God,*
> *but now have received mercy because of their disobedience,*
> *so now, because of the mercy shown to you,*
> *they have proved disobedient,*
> *but only in order that they too may receive mercy.*

Doxology

11.33–36   This splendid doxology, which lifts God far beyond the range of human perception and agency and yet brings him infinitely close, is based upon the wisdom tradition of Israel (movingly displayed in the Book of Job, for example in ch. 28) and the reflections of such Hellenistic philosophers as the Jewish Philo and the Gentile Seneca, Paul's contemporaries. The divine Person is not single-minded or trivial but rich, not rash or insensitive but wise, not uninformed but knowledgeable. Where we are at a loss in making judgments or finding our way, *his judgments* are *inscrutable, his ways unsearchable*. He is therefore not dependent on our information or intercession. We cannot put him under obligation by piety or charity. All that is, has been, and will be, is his creation and care. Hence the service of our God is not harsh, grim, bleak – but splendid.

Spiritual worship
12.1–21

In the third section of the Epistle Paul is more relaxed. He is giving pastoral advice rather than arguing a theological case. He can now take it for granted that God's saving goodness is available through the death and resurrection of Jesus Christ, that both Jews and Gentiles are acceptable to God through faith in him, and that an inescapable change in social awareness has begun. But groups of believers, being accepted by faith, can no longer be confident that responses to God and their neighbours are suitably guided by Mosaic or Hellenistic traditions. So Paul turns to morals and religion in a period of social change when it is high time to wake out of sleep (13.11).

12.1–2   He begins with worship – and it is discerning worship, (as the Greek says: REB *worship offered by mind and heart* is a ringing phrase that starts no echo). When he implores them to offer their bodily selves as living agents of God, they are not like people offering animal or human victims because God demands them, nor are they like people observing food prohibitions because it is a command of the Holy One. They are responding to *God's mercy* and comprehend what they are doing. They are offering their (bodily) selves – in contrast to the degradation of their bodies in 1.24 – in *a living sacrifice* to God, *dedicated and fit for his acceptance*. A sacrifice is something wholly dedicated to God. Obviously *a living sacrifice* is worship that offers a living, not a dead, object and hence brings the worshipper new possibilities of living.

This kind of worship encourages nonconformity towards the present age and transformation by thinking in new ways. Since the *present world* (or age) is undergoing change because God wills it so, Christians must not take refuge in the world as it was but must confidently move forward and *discern the will of God, what is good, acceptable and perfect* (in the sense of completely appropriate) in each new situation.

12.3–5   Relying on God's generosity in making him an apostle (as

he said at the beginning of the Epistle 1.5, and will say again later
15.15), Paul expects them to move forward confidently indeed, but
not arrogantly. Individual Christians are not allowed an optimistic
or aggressive self-assessment but are to *form a sober estimate* of themselves. That refers to one of the four ancient moral virtues (moderation, together with wisdom, courage, and justice in Plato's *Republic*
427d) and probably sounds boring to modern ears. But sobriety
implies no panic, no wild excitement but a sensible and persuasive
estimate. For Paul this moderation is balanced by faith or confidence.
Christians do not put confidence in themselves unless they are
prompted by God and supported by members of his church. Faith is
the common property of the church and God has dealt to each
member a special responsibility for maintaining faith and making it
effective. The Christian community is like a human body *with many
limbs and organs, all with different functions*, all depending on the
others – as Paul had earlier worked out when writing to Corinth
(I Cor. 12).

12.6–16   This section therefore describes how gifts are exercised in
the community so that they remain gifts of *God's grace* and both
confirm and promote the community's faith. The word 'grace' has
already appeared frequently in the theological argument where it
means God's generosity to sinful and needy people who turn to him
in faith. We live by grace (5.2) not by our own efforts but by God's
help. Grace established its reign (5.21), i.e. it is the dominant
influence in the Christian community and the source of *different gifts
allotted to each of us by God's grace*. Examples are now given, with
interesting qualifications: (*a*) *inspired utterance* but only in accordance
with faith in Christ; (*b*) *administration, teaching, counselling* – each gift
confined to its own proper sphere and not interfering with others;
and (*c*) charitable giving *without grudging*, leading *with enthusiasm,
cheerfully* helping *others in distress*.
   The words in that list have a variety of meanings, and diverse
translations are available. But even as they stand they give an
interesting impression of an early Christian church. Its leading
characteristic is inspired intelligible speech. Under the influence of
the Spirit there are people in direct contact with God. Prompted by
him they say what needs to be said, in their particular situation,
about the Christian tradition brought to them by apostles and
evangelists. The church is located on the social map by horizontal
and vertical co-ordinates. That being so, *administration* is needed
because the community must do more than simply exist and protect
itself: it must respond to God's promptings. (Consider the necessary

administration for Paul to collect the supportive fund for hard-pressed Christians in Jerusalem and to take it there (15.31).) *Teaching* is needed to convey the pattern of Christian believing, including what Paul called 'my way of life in Christ, something I teach everywhere in all the churches' (I Cor. 4.17). How much there was to learn is suggested by Paul's use and interpretation of scripture (p. 101). And this would not be something to be learnt once for all and accepted; it would be a Christian version of continuing education and discovery. And then there would be *counselling*: giving support to perplexed and distressed Christians, standing by them, perhaps indicating the way forward when they were fearful or showing them the way back if they were in fault but repentant. And if perhaps in administration they gave to charity, then *give without grudging*; if perhaps they took the lead in teaching, then *lead with enthusiasm*; if as counsellors they *help others in distress, do it cheerfully*.

These words are addressed to the whole community (v. 3) not to the leader or leaders. Indeed the rather throw-away reference to 'leader' in verse 8 suggests no single leader of the community but various members taking leadership as occasion demanded. Paul's moral teaching is not centred upon community officers applying rules but upon Christians behaving in such and such ways – in fact, in ways required by *love*. The Greek language, like our own, had a large stock of words for the notion of love, some of which are present in such words as erotic, philanthropic, sympathy, and zeal. The New Testament used five of them. To indicate God's love Paul chose the word *agapē*, that was rather colourless and seldom used in ordinary Greek (and has merely a minor technical use in English for the *agapē* or love-feast). But he could therefore fill it with his powerful conviction of God's love in Christ for sinful people (5.5, 8; 8.35, 39). Paul now uses that very word for human love within the Christian community. Verse 9 announces the theme: sincere *love*. Then follow descriptive phrases, almost like notes for a long speech, building up an impression with energy and rhetorical skill of what genuine love requires. Towards the end, at a specially significant point, description changes to instruction (though translations assume that Paul is giving instructions throughout).

Love implies strongly affectionate feelings and activities. Affection can be spontaneous or it may develop. Its genuineness or sincerity cannot be commanded but it can be tested, even encouraged, by the activities that belong to it. So sincere love is discriminating, distinguishing between good and evil – and firmly taking sides (v. 9). It is mutual, excluding self promotion (v. 10). It is energetic, *aglow with the Spirit* in serving the Lord – if indeed that is what Paul wrote. *Serve the Lord* is an oddly vague instruction, and it is possible that Paul wrote 'serving the time' as in a small number of ancient sources. (The word for Lord is *kyrio*, for time *kairo*.) The familiar meaning of 'time-serving', in ancient times as in ours, is changing your views to suit prevailing fashion. Here that is clearly wrong: if Paul wrote 'time' with the significance it has in 13.11, then he expected Christian love to respond to opportunities presented by the radical changes now beginning (v. 11). Genuine love is practical and encouraging, persisting *in prayer* to learn how to act and to *stand firm* (vv. 12–13). It must be unresentful towards *persecutors* (here the descriptive words become commands) and *call down blessings* on them. Had not Paul himself been a persecutor, and then yielded to the divine blessing?

This instruction echoes the commands of Jesus in Matt. 5.43–44 and Luke 6.27–28 (v. 14). Finally love seeks agreement, it seeks a common aim (as Paul will say in 15.5). Christians do not set their minds on high matters but are fully occupied with matters that by Greek standards seem servile, menial, and petty. *Do not keep thinking how wise you are.* In that exposition we have departed from the REB translation: *Be ready to mix with humble people* which suggests, to modern ears at least, that Paul and the Roman Christians were given to middle-class snobbery. There are two problems here: (*a*) Paul uses a word that could mean either servile things or servile people. Most frequently it refers to people and it may do so here, but the words immediately preceding certainly refer to high matters, not people. (*b*) To Greek sensibilities the word indicated debased people and things, to be dismissed from consideration; to Jewish sensibilities it indicated what needed protection and encouragement, as often in the Psalms. There is a fine example in the apocryphal book Judith 9.11 (in Maccabaean times, some two hundred years before Paul): 'You are the God of the humble, the help of the poor, the support of the weak, the protector of the despairing, the deliverer of those who have lost all hope.' That may have been in Paul's mind.

12.17–21   In verse 14 Paul has indicated responses within the Christian community to persecution from outside. In 12.17–13.10 he turns to the community's external relations and ends by bringing both inner life and outward responses under the rule of love.

Even if Christians have to endure unpleasantness from the outside world, they are to follow the Jewish wisdom tradition and not retaliate in kind. There is an echo of the Greek version of Prov. 3.4: 'Take thought for what is good before the Lord and men.' As far as they can, they are to live peaceably with everybody, not seeking revenge but leaving a place for the anger (i.e. God's active resistance to wickedness – see pp. 8 and 36) for *'vengeance is mine, says the Lord, I will repay'* (an adaptation of Deut. 32.35 in the Song of Moses, as translated in NRSV). That is to say, Christians have no business with vengeance. That is for God alone, and is not in our hands. The same thing is implied in verse 20 which quotes Prov. 25.21–22: *'If your enemy is hungry, feed him; if he is thirsty, give him a drink*; so far so good, but what are we to make of the next words? – *by doing this you will heap live coals on his head.'* It is usually said that the *live coals* are a symbol of burning remorse. But a hostile person could easily interpret kindness as weakness. In any case, is Christian kindness only an attempt to embarrass the enemy? Another suggestion is that carrying live coals in a pot on the head is an obscure and grotesque Egyptian ritual of repentance. Can you imagine the congregation at Rome understanding that? But if some of them at least knew the Hebrew scriptures (as Paul certainly expected) they would recognize *live coals* as a vivid symbol of the divine anger: 'The earth shook and quaked … shaking because of his anger … glowing coals and searing heat' (Ps. 18.7–8, which is the same as II Sam. 22.8–9). The Psalmist begs God to protect him from enemies: 'Let burning coals be rained on them' (Ps. 140.10). Whatever Paul's quotation meant to the composer of Proverbs, to Paul it meant: be generous to your opponent, for vengeance is no business of yours. If God thinks fit, the divine anger will be heaped on him. Not particularly *on his head*, of course, since 'head' means person, as commonly in Greek. As one example out of many: 'The Lord will bring back his bloody deeds on his own head' I Kings 2.32 NRSV which REB correctly renders 'The Lord will hold him responsible for his own death.' Paul is saying: You act kindly; leaving God's anger to deal amply with your enemy. *Use good to conquer evil*.

The civil authorities
13.1–10

13.1–7   That instruction leads on at once to the relations between the Christian community and the civil authorities. If Paul was right in thinking that Jews and Gentiles were being drawn together in Christ, and that a major change in social awareness had begun and would soon become irresistible (as in 13.11–14), then Christians must know how they stood as regards civil affairs. From what is said in verse 7 it seems possible that some were asking why taxes should still be paid if a new day was dawning. But Paul insists on respect for and obedience to the civil authority. On that two things must be said. (*a*) He is saying nothing new when he asserts that *the existing authorities are instituted by* God. That was the standard Jewish view. 'Through me kings hold sway and governors enact just laws. Through me princes wield authority, from me all rulers on earth derive their rank' (Prov. 8.15–16). If rulers misbehave, that can be dealt with. Wisdom addresses rulers of the multitude: 'Your authority was bestowed on you by the Lord, your power comes from the Most High. He will probe your actions and scrutinize your intentions … Swiftly and terribly he will descend on you, for judgment falls relentlessly on those in high places' (Wisd. 6.1–5). Just as Christians are not to take vengeance for personal injury, so they are not to rebel against authority, whatever the pressure. (*b*) Paul was not laying down a general rule about *authorities in power* at every time and place, but was speaking about the response of Roman Christians to Roman rule at the particular time when (as he saw it) one world was passing away and another was being born. We mistake the authority of scripture if we assume that its statements (or at least those that appeal to us) are universally valid. As Paul himself says 'The scriptures written long ago were all written for our instruction' (15.4) so that, encouraged by the ancient response of faith, we may work out our own response now.

The opening words are carefully chosen to emphasize a concern for order – as this rewrite of the Greek will show:

Every person must be subordinate *to the authorities in power,*

for all authority comes from God,
and the existing authorities are ordered *by him.*
It follows that anyone who is insubordinate to *authority*
is resisting the orders of God,
and insubordinate people *have themselves to thank,* and so on.

In Paul's view the Roman administration maintained an ordered structure of society (not necessarily one that was fair or kind) which would permit the corporate lives of Jew and Gentile to be united in Christ. When a few years later the Jews revolted against Rome, that union became impossible.

Paul is saying the dutiful things – with what we might call a poker face – about Roman officials, from those who *hold the power of the sword* (capital punishment) and so are of high rank to local administrators of taxes and levies. Such dutiful remarks may stand the church in good stead if the authorities become hostile; and in any case the majority of people could have little influence on government (as was indeed so until the mid-nineteenth century in Britain). The authorities are *instituted* by God, *God's agents* for the common good and for punishing offenders. (In verse 4 NRSV has 'to execute wrath on the wrongdoer'. This is one way of making the divine anger effective: see p. 107). Only wrongdoers will *fear them; governments hold no terrors for the law-abiding but only for the criminal.*

That remark purports to be an approving description, but it is in fact an accusation. *Pay tax and levy, reverence and respect, to those to whom they are due.* But to whom are they due? To authorities who give approval to the law-abiding, and hand criminals over to the consequences of their wrong-doing; to governments whose actions raise no objection from your *conscience.* But few governments pass those tests. Many governments abuse law-abiding people and treat them cruelly because they can be exploited for the benefit of the rich and powerful. Paul's insistence that the authorities are instituted by God brings them into the world of religion. The slogan 'Keep religion out of politics' disregards Paul – and indeed much of the biblical tradition. In describing the authority, Paul uses two terms familiar in Hellenistic life for civic officials and public servants: one is 'deacon' (v. 4, translated as *agents,* which is also the description of Phoebe in 16.1) and the other is 'minister' (v. 6, translated as *in God's service,* which is also Paul's self-description in 15.16 'a minister of Christ Jesus to the Gentiles'). Paul and Phoebe were what they were because the civil administration had crucified Jesus Christ, and in no sense were Roman officials to be regarded as Christian ministers. Nevertheless they were servants and agents of God who needed the support, reverence and respect of Christians, in so far as the civil administration itself was true to its calling. When long afterwards it became possible for the majority to influence government, Paul's view of the God-given nature of government requires Christians to be concerned with public order, the reward of goodness and the restraint of wickedness, the conscientious examination of laws, and even the purpose, size, and proper use of taxes.

13.8–10   Taxes are an obligation, but so is love. Not only family love, or love for one another in the Christian community (described in 12.9–16), but the practice of love in the wider community. Love for one's *neighbour* (as in vv. 9 and 10) indeed, so long as *neighbour* carries the meaning of fellow human being, the other person (as in v. 8). To most of us *neighbour* still has a smallish local reference; but with modern communications' techniques, the other person may be both far away and in intimate contact.

To make his point, Paul uses the second part of the Ten Commandments (Ex. 20.2–17; Deut. 5.6–21). The first part confines worship to the God. who brought Israel out of Egypt, prohibits images and the wrong use of the divine name, and establishes the Sabbath. Since that would be distractive for a mixed Jew and Gentile congregation – and in any case God is now defined as the Lord who raised Christ on the first day of the week – nothing is here said about duty to God or the cultic rules of the Instruction. Of the six Commandments in the second part Paul cites no adultery, murder, theft, or coveting. The order is unimportant: it varied in a number of ancient sources. The omissions (respect for parents, malice towards neighbours) were probably thought too domestic; but Paul rather grandly waves his hand and says – '*and any other commandment there may be* (in this area of community behaviour) *are all summed up in the one rule, Love your neighbour as yourself*'.

That rule from Lev. 19.18 comes from one of the more heart-warming chapters of the book, something like the Ten Command-ments applied to everyday life. Thus harvesters are to leave enough for the poor to gather; no stealing, cheating or deceiving of your neighbour; wages are to be promptly paid; no contemptuous unconcern for the deaf and blind; respect for the aged; and a foreigner is to be treated as a native born – 'love him as yourself, because you were aliens in Egypt'. Before Paul's Epistle it seems that explicit reference to Lev. 19.18 is not found in Jewish writings, but they certainly express the conviction that love for God and neigh-bour are the basis of Jewish life. In a collection of imagined farewell speeches by the forefathers of Israel, the Testament of the Twelve

Patriarchs (perhaps a hundred years or more before Paul), that conviction is present, e.g. 'Throughout all your life love the Lord, and one another with a true heart' (Test. Dan. 5.3). It was standard Jewish teaching that human beings are made in the image of God, so that an offence against a human being is disregard of God. According to Mark 12.28–34 Jesus defined the primary commandments as love of God according to Deut. 6.5 and love of neighbour according to Lev. 19.18 – and a Jewish scribe agreed with him. So Paul is well within Jewish tradition; but whereas Jewish teachers accepted love of neighbour as the commandment from which all other commandments could be deduced, so implying the necessity of obedience to all other commandments, Paul used love of neighbour to indicate the manner in which any rule should be carried out. Hence his sensitive treatment of the problems disclosed in chapters 14–15.

Hence love cannot wrong a neighbour. That negative form is more practical than the positive. If you are a conscientious Christian and are told to love your neighbour you will start searching for loving activities – wondering how far you should go, wondering whether you will irritate rather than help, possibly causing offence by implying criticism, and so on. Loving your neighbour demands a good deal of mutual respect, confidence, and frankness. On the other hand, if you say 'That would hurt my neighbour' you may be on safer ground. And such love may be *the fulfilment of the law* or (in the more helpful earlier phrase) it may meet *every requirement of the law*.

Salvation is near

13.11–14

13.11–14   This comprehensive practice of love is to be your aim as you *remember that this is the hour of crisis*. Other translations are less alarmist: NRSV has 'the moment to wake out of sleep'. *Hour of crisis* represents a time word (meaning not length of time but appropriate time) which Paul has used more than once already, e.g. in 8.18 'the sufferings we now endure'. To us *crisis* means a decisive moment of great difficulty with the risk of danger. Perhaps Paul had that feeling. He told his readers to 'conform no longer to the pattern of the present world' (12.2) and he may have urged them to serve the present critical time (12.11; see p. 106). They are to wake up to the change that is about to take place. *Deliverance* (from ancient hostilities towards God and rival human communities) *is nearer to us than it was when we first believed* (i.e. became Christians). *It is far on in the night; day is near* – imagery that has deep roots in Jewish expectation.

> These are the words of the Lord:
> In the time of my favour I answered you;
> on the day of deliverance I came to your aid.
> I have formed you, and destined you
> to be a light for peoples …
> I said to the prisoners, 'Go free',
> and to those in darkness, 'Come out into the open' (Isa. 49.8–9).

In the Old Testament there are sixteen references to the Day of the Lord, mostly promising God's devastating warfare against Israel's enemies (only Amos suggests that there may be devastating consequences for Israel as well). Paul makes standard references to that Day in 2.5 and 16; and in possibly his earliest letter the imagery of the suddenly-occurring Day of the Lord is strongly developed, with the alert Christian 'armed with the breastplate of faith and love, and the hope of salvation for a helmet (I Thess. 5.2–11). To the Romans Paul says *Let Christ Jesus himself be the armour that you wear*. In other words, when night turns to day, the Lord will bring in major changes and there will be a fight – in which Christians will take part.

But their only protection will be their faith in Christ, and their rules of engagement will be his rules. We are to *behave with decency as befits the day*, not with the indecencies that are commonplace in most social groups. Paul gives an extract from his more comprehensive list in Gal. 5.19–21 of what used to be called sins of the flesh. They are sinful because people use the power of being in a group to dominate and suborn members, so as to set up *quarrels or jealousies*, to go beyond all enjoyment and safety in riotous behaviour, drunkenness, group sex, and debauchery. Two examples from the ancient world: (*a*) riotous behaviour: 'The Gentiles filled the temple with licentious revelry; they took their pleasure with prostitutes and had intercourse with women in the sacred precincts' II Macc. 6.4; (*b*) A bad servant 'says to himself "The master is a long time coming", and begins to bully the other servants and to eat and drink with his drunken friends' Matt. 24.48–49. How dreadful human beings are when their chief social pleasures are cruelty and group sex! *Give your* flesh *no opportunity to satisfy its desires*.

What Paul expected to happen when day succeeded night is not clear. Certainly he expected Jews and Gentiles to change their minds about the relations of their communities to one another, to God, and to morality. But would there be any significant *happening*? In previous Epistles Paul had used the vivid language of waiting expectantly for God's Son from heaven, bringing the dead with him and saving us from the wrath to come (I Thess. 1.10; 4.14–18). The day of the Lord is transferred from our God to Jesus (I Thess. 5.2; I Cor. 1.7–8; 3.13), so 'wait until the Lord comes. He will bring to light what darkness hides and disclose our inner motives' (I Cor. 4.5). There is even a planned and orderly scheme for resurrection, beginning with Christ, then at his coming, those who belong to Christ, and so on (I Cor. 15.22–26). 'The day of Christ Jesus' appears again in Phil. 1.6, 10, an Epistle probably written after Romans.

But in Romans itself the day of the Lord Jesus is nowhere mentioned, and nothing is said about his coming from heaven. Is he not interceding for us at God's right hand (Rom. 8.34)? We shall be saved through Christ from the Anger but by his life, not specifically by his coming (Rom. 5.9–10). Is it not likely that the coming of God's Son from heaven is as much metaphorical as the grafting in of the wild olive? Some Christians at Thessalonica must have supposed so because they thought it was already here (II Thess. 2.2), and a similar view at Corinth may explain some Christians' assertion that there is no resurrection of the dead (I Cor. 15.12). Is it not likely that the coming from heaven must be metaphorical if it is to have continuing theological validity? Perhaps so! But Paul expected something to happen. 'We exult in the hope of the divine glory that is to be ours' – 'the glory, as yet unrevealed, which is in store for us' (5.2; 8.18). What does Paul imply, towards the end of the Epistle, when he says that he has completed the preaching of the gospel of Christ from Jerusalem as far round as Illyricum, and must soon set out for Spain? Is he not working towards an apostolic dead-line? If our own Christianity is to be apostolic, must we not always be anticipating the end of the present phase and preparing ourselves for the next?

Mutual acceptance
14.1–15.13

14.1–12 But whatever the expected happening, it was not going to happen yet – and Paul had been informed of difficulties among the Roman Christians. With a mixed community of Jews and Gentiles that was not surprising. The Jews had recently been in trouble with the authorities: 'Claudius had issued an edict that all Jews should leave Rome' (Acts 18.2) probably in AD 49, though how effective was the edict and how long it lasted, nobody knows. How could Christian Jews defend themselves against fellow Jews if they failed to buy meat that was kosher and wine that was tithed, if they abandoned Sabbath and the festivals? Or perhaps the perplexities of 'meat consecrated to an idol' (I Cor. 8 and 10) had upset Rome as well as Corinth. Or perhaps this was not a Jewish problem at all but the propaganda of an ascetic Hellenistic sect that longed for the devout simple life. It does not greatly matter that we cannot confidently identify the particular features: the main point is that some are *weak in faith*. Not that they lack faith, but their faith needs support to convince themselves (and perhaps others) that they indeed possess faith.

Paul's persuasive rhetoric becomes more accessible to modern readers if his presumptions, examples, and conclusions are set out in logical order. Thus, God has accepted each Christian as his household servant (v. 3) – which is the meaning of 'justification' – so that *whether he stands or falls is his own Master's business*, and he will take care of that (v. 4). In the end *we shall all stand before God's tribunal*, as Isa. 45.23 indicates (vv. 10–11). Hence each Christian *will be answerable to God* (v. 12). Thus it is that *none of us lives, and equally none of us dies for himself* alone (i.e. without reference to others). Living or dying we are responsible to the Lord and we belong to the lordship that was achieved by Christ's death and resurrection (vv. 7–9). Now consider the question about permissible food. Some of you *have faith strong enough to eat all kinds of food* (v. 2) and when they *eat meat they give thanks to God* and so *honour the Lord* (v. 6). Others among you, being weaker in faith, eat *only vegetables* (v. 2) but they *have the Lord in mind when abstaining, since they too give thanks to*

God (v. 6). To take another example, *some make a distinction between this day and that; others regard all days alike. Everyone must act on his own convictions* but, in any case, *those who honour the day honour the Lord* (vv. 5–6). *Why* then (if you are not confident in faith) *pass judgment on your fellow-Christian?* Or (if you are confident in faith) *why do you look down on your fellow-Christian?* (v. 10). So this is the rule: *Accept anyone who is weak in faith, without debate about his misgivings* (v. 1). However much the church may have to give thought to such problems, *those who eat meat must not look down on those who do not, and those who do not eat meat must not pass judgment on those who do* (v. 3). That argument has secured for individual believers a highly personal responsibility to the Lord. *Everyone must act on his own convictions* or (as NRSV translates) 'Let all be fully convinced in their own minds.' But that is asking a great deal. Our convictions are often a rag-bag of ideas picked up from family and social group, or revolted against. Being fully convinced in our minds implies willingness to weigh up an argument and make decisions. Paul may thus make it possible for Jewish converts to decide against the ancient practices of Israel, but it does not protect them from pressures experienced in membership of their new Jewish-Gentile Christian community. To that he now turns. Once again it will be instructive to work out the underlying sequence of his thought.

14.13–23   When Paul speaks (not frequently) of *the kingdom of God* he usually mentions who or what does not belong to it. Here it means in effect the practical obligations of being the people of God – hence not matters of *eating and drinking, but justice* (i.e. acceptable community behaviour), *peace, and joy, inspired by the Holy Spirit* (v. 17). *Everyone who shows himself a servant of Christ in this way is acceptable to God and approved by men* (v. 18). The Christian life is indeed distinctive but it is not dominated by a need to assert and maintain separation from others.

Paul now asserts his own conviction, as of one confident in faith: *All that I know of the Lord Jesus convinces me that nothing* (i.e. no kind of food) *is impure in itself; only, if anyone considers something impure, then for him it is impure* (v. 14). *Everything is pure in itself, but it is wrong to eat if by eating you cause another to stumble. Do not destroy the work of God* (i.e. the Christian community) *for the sake of food* (v. 20). *Place no obstacle or stumbling block in a fellow-Christian's way* (v. 13). You *must not let what you think good be brought into disrepute* (v. 16). *If your fellow-Christian is outraged by what you eat, then you are no longer guided by love. Do not by your eating be the ruin of one for whom Christ died!* (v. 15) *It is right to abstain from eating meat or drinking wine or from anything else which causes a fellow-Christian to stumble. If you have some firm conviction, keep it between yourself and God. Anyone who can make his decision without misgivings is fortunate. But anyone who has misgivings and yet eats is guilty, because his action does not arise from conviction, and anything that does not arise from conviction is sin* (vv. 21–23). The REB translation of verse 23 removes the possibility of the absurd (but ancient) conclusion that everything done by non-Christians is wicked. Paul clearly means that a Christian who is led, by the example of other Christians, to do what he thinks to be wrong is being led into sin. Christians are free to do what they confidently believe to be right, but they can give up that freedom – permanently or on appropriate occasions – if they are in danger of leading less confident Christians into sin.

What was this eating of meat, drinking of wine, and perhaps observation of special days that proved so upsetting that lives might be ruined and the church pulled apart? The problem does not exactly correspond to the suggestions on p. 115: we do not know, and perhaps it does not matter since the corresponding problems in our own time are so different.

Why in our day are questions of eating and drinking a matter of Christian concern? (*a*) We have Jewish and Muslim neighbours, and some Christian sects prohibit certain kinds of food and drink. (*b*) Some substances are drugs, including alcohol, and socially dangerous. (*c*) Some foods are personally dangerous to health. (*d*) Some foods are morally objectionable because produced by firms exploiting third world needs or by countries governed by unsavoury regimes. (*e*) Much meat, especially cheap meat in quantity, is morally objectionable because it exploits cruelty to animals. (*f*) By and large our lives are held together by a familiar diet: we are overcome with caution by anything foreign and unusual, with panic by anything outlandish. As for Paul, it is clear that his problems were not ours; but he may remind us that food has something to do with responsibility to God and our neighbours. Our choice of food (granted that we are among the lucky ones who have choice of food, indeed who have food at all) is not settled by advertising, hypermarkets, and the food industry. Paul's next words are perhaps appropriate, at least if we are among the lucky ones.

15.1–6   Paul now clearly identifies himself with the *strong*, the confident in faith, not to assert his rights but to show that an apostolic minister knows better than anyone how to renounce privilege. Those who are confident in faith are not to act simply to please themselves, but to act for the constructive good of their neighbour. This ruling is supported by the constitutive example of Christ who *did not please himself*, namely by dying as he did. The *words of scripture* are Ps. 69.9 where hostility towards God falls upon the devout and anguished sufferer – thus allowing another verse to appear in the Gospel passion narrative. Paul has already used the psalm at 11.9–10, and here he might appropriately have quoted: 'Let none who seek you be humiliated through me' (v. 6). The whole psalm should be studied for its expression of acute misery, unacceptable anger, and final confidence. Disconcerting as this may be, the scriptures encourage *perseverance*, offer *encouragement*, and lead to *hope* – as God himself does. The hope is that the Christian community will *praise the God and Father of our Lord Jesus Christ* with a common intention.

15.7–13   We draw to a conclusion. The section 14.1–15.6 has been devoted to the mutual acceptance of two somewhat divergent groups, the strong in faith and the weak, in the Roman church. This now broadens out to the mutual acceptance of Jew and Gentile in the church. They are *to accept one another as Christ accepted* them, *to the glory of God*. He performed a double service: fulfilling God's promise to the patriarchs of a saviour for the Jewish people, and making it possible for the Gentiles *to glorify God for his mercy* – as passages of scripture had said they would. Paul has a string of quotations: first Ps. 18.49 in verse 9, seemingly a most unsuitable psalm which says 'because my conduct was spotless in his eyes, the Lord rewarded me as my righteousness deserved' (vv. 20–24) – which Paul over-turned in his teaching of justification by faith. The end of the psalm (vv. 44–48) shows contempt for foreigners and pleads for vengeance against them – which Paul also overturns in his conviction that there is no distinction between Jew and Greek in justification by faith (Rom. 10.11–13). The second scriptural quotation in verse 10 is from the Song of Moses in Deut. 32.43, satisfactory if the vengeful Hebrew text is discarded for the Greek version: 'Rejoice with him you heavens, and let all the sons of God worship him. *Gentiles, join in celebration with his people,* and grow strong with him all the angels of God.' The third quotation in verse 11 is entirely apt, from Ps. 117.1 referring to God's protecting love and faithfulness. The last quotation in verse 12 is from Isaiah 11.10 standing at the end of a passage describing the ideal king, marked by wisdom, resolution, and piety. The prophet looked forward to a day when a new shoot (*scion*) from the root-stock *of Jesse* (the father of King David) should *come to govern the Gentiles*. For Paul, harking back to 'a descendant of David' in 1.3, that day has come.

It should be clear that Paul was not appealing to these quotations to prove his theological convictions, but was showing how, with those convictions, scripture – the Instruction, the Prophets, and the Writings – could be read. Deuteronomy 32 could support Paul's theology if read not in the Hebrew but in the Greek tradition; Isa. 11 if it was lifted out of its original historical situation and applied to Paul's day; Ps. 18 if its strong prejudices were contradicted, in the knowledge that Ps. 117 would see Paul safe home. With Paul you cannot talk naively about the authority of scripture but only about the authority of the Spirit, who is the Spirit of Christ (8.9), applied to scripture.

There is a concluding prayer of mutual acceptance. The *life of faith* in a God who works by death and resurrection is based on *hope* – confident expectation. Remember Abraham in an impossible situation (4.18); hope of recovering the divine glory (5.2); being put to the test and ending with a hope that does not shame us (5.4–5); the hope of creation being set free (8.20–21); hope that keeps us joyful (12.12); the encouragement of the scriptures to maintain hope and perseverance (15.4) – *until by the power of the Holy Spirit, you overflow with hope.*

Rome's importance in Paul's plans
15.14–33

At last Paul resumes the formal beginning of the Epistle in 1.8–15 which mentioned his 'eagerness to declare the gospel to you in Rome'. That community is *full of goodness, equipped with knowledge of every kind, well able to give advice to one another*. It is a competent, autonomous community. An apostle uses tact and cannot domineer. They must make their own decisions. But because of the gift he had from God, Paul writes to remind them of something. Of what? Probably of the conditions on which Gentiles can become Christian. Paul is *a minister of Christ Jesus to the Gentiles in the* priestly *service of the gospel of God*, so that the offering of the Gentiles may be acceptable, *consecrated by the Holy Spirit*. The REB translation of verse 15 has been brought closer to the Greek so that we can consider what Paul actually said: 'the offering of the Gentiles' is ambiguous. It could mean 'the offering that the Gentiles make'; or possibly 'the Gentiles regarded as an offering', which is what REB intends. What could it mean? 'We have captured the Gentiles and made them (Jewish) Christians like ourselves.' The great missionary movement of modern times worked on those lines. Fifty years ago ministers in West Africa wore clerical collars and black suits, despite the splendid garments of their own tradition. Christian congregations were taught to sing European type hymns which in a tonal language are inappropriate and sometimes meaningless. Devoted missionaries captured the hearts of many West Africans and offered them to God in the European image, instead of encouraging them to find African offerings appropriate to Christ. The latter was Paul's aim. If you offer a gift to someone, the manner of offering the gift is sometimes as important as the gift itself. A priest is someone who knows the appropriate offering and the right way to make it. When Gentiles became Christians (by faith, not by law fulfilment) they had many gifts to offer God – some suitable, some inappropriate. Their specially-appointed apostle says: 'I have self-confidence ("I have grounds for pride" is the complacent remark of a chairman's report) *in Christ Jesus* as regards the proper approach to God. But I would not dare to say anything except what Christ has achieved *through me to bring the Gentiles into his allegiance, by word and* deed ("I have spoken and things happened"), *by the power of signs and portents* (the standard Old Testament idiom for what happens when people are brought out of slavery into freedom), *and by the power of the Holy Spirit.'*

But what next should Paul do? He had *completed the preaching of the gospel of Christ from Jerusalem as far round as Illyricum*. If you have a modern map of the eastern Mediterranean you could be shown places attached to Paul in a great arc from Israel, through Turkey, southern Greece to Greek Macedonia (15.26), but not further north, i.e. not Albania and the remaining east coast of the Adriatic, which was the ancient Illyricum. The evidence is in the addresses of Paul's Epistles and Acts 7–28. It is an enormous area in which to *have completed the preaching of the gospel of Christ*, even if he went only as far as the border of Illyricum; even if he was not the only evangelist at work and Paul made a point of *taking the gospel to places where the name of Christ had not been heard, not wanting to build on another man's foundation* (v. 20). Three things become plain about Paul as an evangelist: (*a*) even though he is the apostle of the Gentiles he does not regard them as his property and power base; (*b*) he really does trust the newly-formed Christian communities to evangelize neighbouring areas; and (*c*) *as scripture says* (Isa. 52.15, the beginning of the poem about the Suffering Servant) he was prepared to preach Christ when 'many Gentiles recoil at the sight of him, and kings curl their lips in disgust' as Isaiah said.

He has been prevented from visiting Rome by the task described in verses 19–20. He regards himself as a sort of ombudsman for the Gentiles, making sure that they are not under pressure to come in as pseudo-Jewish Christians. He has set up his markers and must now move on. His mind is on Spain: there is an area to be opened up before the expected great shift of understanding takes place in the Roman world. Not surprisingly he wants to visit Rome, the centre of the Gentile world, and to involve Rome in his apostolic perception of the forthcoming change. But he also wants to involve them in Jerusalem, the centre of the Jewish world to which they owe the essential perceptions of their faith in Christ. Almost certainly their involvement would require them to support his journey to Spain with escorts and guide, but before that to support with prayer his *errand to Jerusalem*. To do so they must understand what is at stake. The Christians of *Macedonia and Achaia have resolved to raise a fund for the benefit of the poor among God's people at Jerusalem* (v. 26). On the principle that members of a family look after their kindred in need, the Gentile Christians of Greece are claiming the family privilege of supporting Jewish Christians in Jerusalem. In order that a fund for *material needs* should not seem an embarrassing return for *spiritual treasures*, Paul himself is taking the gifts, but he is not at all sure what the response will be. No doubt there will be Jewish opponents, and probably Jewish Christian opponents as well, not at all convinced by Paul's determination that Gentile Christians must not be required to accept rules of the Mosaic Instruction. This fund was not a recent project: in earlier days the Jerusalem apostles had agreed separate areas of evangelism with Paul on condition that he should 'keep in mind the poor', which he always made it his business to do (Gal. 2.10); and some of the practical arrangements are mentioned in I Cor. 16.1–4 and II Cor. 8.19–21. But Luke's description of Paul's arrival in Jerusalem says nothing about the fund or its reception, and there is merely a passing mention of 'charitable gifts' in one of Paul's speeches of self-defence (Acts 21.17–26; 24.17). According to Luke, the Jerusalem Christians claimed to have 'many thousands of converts … among the Jews, all of them staunch upholders of the law', and the 'new way', as it was called, was well known to the Roman authorities. But even though Paul was under arrest, and at Caesarea open arrest, for two years, Luke says nothing about support from the Christians (Acts 21.20; 24.22–23, 27). Whatever may be thought about the accuracy or selectivity of Luke's story, it seems likely that the fund was not a success, that Paul went to Rome as a prisoner and was welcomed there by fellow-Christians (Acts 28.14–15). Luke ends his story with Paul 'openly and without hindrance' preaching the gospel. Whether he was then released and went to Spain is quite unknown.

The enormous care that Paul devoted to the fund, the good intentions of Greek Christians uniting concern for the poor and respect for the mother church, ended in some kind of disaster. For Paul it led to imprisonment, the end of far-flung, imaginative evangelism, and probably death. But this is what Christians may expect if they serve a God who works by death and resurrection. Paul's great mission field 'from Jerusalem as far round as Illyricum' and across the sea to Rome shrank in size, perception, and confidence – but within a century his Epistles were at the centre of Western Christianity, and his thought has permeated all subsequent theology.

One more observation is necessary. Even an apostle, even *the* apostle of the Gentiles, can be full of apprehension, not knowing whether he *may find acceptance with God's people*. Appealing not to a church that he has founded but to the Christians of Rome he wants their *support*, he wants to *enjoy* their *company for a while*, he wants *allies in the fight* that is likely, he wants to *enjoy a time of rest with them*, to find in their company *the God of peace*. Can we not say *Amen* to all that?

Greetings to the community
16.1–16

Since Paul sends greetings to twenty-eight people by name it is not surprising that he longs for their support. But it is perhaps surprising that he has so many friends in a church he had neither founded nor visited. Ephesus (it has been suggested) would be a more likely congregation (Acts 18–19). Is it possible that copies of Romans were sent to Pauline churches and that we possess the copy sent to Ephesus with appropriate local greetings? It must be admitted that ancient manuscripts of the Epistle display some oddities. For example, the doxology in verses 25–27 sometimes turns up at the end of chapter 14, once at the end of chapter 15. And the grace at the end of verse 20 sometimes appears as verse 24 (omitted from modern translations), sometimes at the end of verse 27. This technical information makes it fairly certain that when Romans was copied in the early centuries of the church, its ending (no longer relevant) was shortened and tidied up; but the ingenious Ephesian proposal has rightly not gathered support. On the other hand, the list of names has provoked growing interest.

16.1–2   Paul gives Phoebe, who perhaps carried the Epistle, an introduction to the community in Rome. She is *a minister in the church at Cenchreae* (the eastern port of Corinth). Paul's word for her is 'deacon' which means servant or helper (perhaps a little more formal in 'the bishops and deacons' in Phil. 1.1). Instead of *good friend* NRSV has 'benefactor': she was a woman of influence and wealth, taking responsibility in the church, helping out the apostle himself, and commended as a suitable delegate to Christians in Rome.

16.3–5   The Jewish wife and husband, Prisca and Aquila, are old associates of Paul. He first met them at Corinth when they had left Rome because of the edict of Claudius against Roman Jews (Acts 18.1 – and see also 18.18–28). They are now back in Rome and an *ecclesia* meets in their house. Paul is grateful to them, not only because they *risked their necks to save* his *life* (nothing is known about that) but also because they had been prominent in the conversion of

Gentiles such as *Epaenatus*, the *first* Asian *convert to Christ in Asia* (the Roman province in what is now Turkey).

16.6   *Mary who worked so hard for you* – the third woman to be mentioned: there are ten all together, doing the hard work of building up churches.

16.7   *Andronicus and Junia*, fellow Jews who somewhere shared Paul's imprisonment. They are *eminent among the apostles* i.e. an outstanding husband and wife team who were Christians before Paul (perhaps among the five hundred to whom the risen Lord appeared, I Cor. 15.6–7). So, plenty of women were prominent in the church, one is named as deacon, another was an apostle. Junia was eminent among the apostles, not merely outstanding in the eyes of the apostles. Junia is unknown as a male name.

16.8–15   The rest of the list contains many names borne by slaves or freed slaves. Some of them may have been members of the imperial household. Two households are mentioned, implying that their (freed) slaves were Christian: the household of Aristobulus, possibly the grandson of Herod the Great and brother of Agrippa I (v. 10); and the household of Narcissus, possibly the notorious freedman of the Emperor Claudius (v. 11). If Mark's Gospel was written in Rome, the Rufus of verse 13 may be the son of Simon of Cyrene who carried the cross for Jesus, according to Mark 15.21.

More information is available in the technical commentaries, but a profile of the Roman community is emerging. Being a collection of house churches, it bridged (not always successfully) the divide between Jews and Gentiles. Its social composition put it in touch with the political and commercial life of Rome, and with travellers in the eastern half of the empire, not without experience of imprisonment and risks to life. The community could be expected to give helpful consideration to the problems of Judaea and the possibilities of Spain. Its membership included some whose calling went back to the time of Jesus, some of them apostles before Paul, including Junia the wife of Andronicus. Of the twenty-six persons individually mentioned, nine are women, including the hard-working pair Tryphaena and Tryphosa – at a guess, twin sisters named Dainty and Delicate.

16.16   *Greet one another with the* holy *kiss* is what Paul said, as he had said it to the churches at Thessalonica and Corinth. *Kiss of peace* might be justified by I Peter 'Greet one another with a loving kiss.

Peace to you all who belong to Christ.' But the introduction of *kiss of peace* here was presumably NEB support for the introduction of the Peace into new eucharistic liturgies. According to *The Concise Oxford Dictionary* a kiss is 'a sign of love, affection, greeting, or reverence'. The 'holy kiss' is a sign of reverence for the image of God in our fellow-Christians.

A sudden rebuke
16.17–20

Properly speaking the letter has now ended; but as is often the case, some afterthoughts are added on – perhaps by other hands than Paul's. The mood clearly changes: instead of the gentle 'accept one another as Christ accepted us' in 15.7, there is intemperate disapproval of people who are *servants not of Christ our Lord but of their own appetites*, even agents of Satan. Paul can be angry but he always argues; here he simply denounces – and denunciation without effective reasons is self-indulgence. Moreover, in verses 17–20 there are no less than eight linguistic features that are not found elsewhere in Paul. It is possible that the colleagues who are with Paul (mentioned in vv. 21–24), having heard his letter so far, think that he has been too gentle with some members of the Roman community. Unless something more is said, they may become subversive. So perhaps Paul allows them to add a warning, in their own not very illuminating words. We can only guess who they were. Look back to 14.1: Paul tells the Romans to 'accept anyone who is weak in faith without debate about his misgivings'. Perhaps there were some among the strong-in-faith who enjoyed bullying and shaming converts who held food taboos (*simple people*), ungracious libertarians who could be denounced as serving *their own appetites*. Perhaps Paul allowed such a sharp criticism to be made: the advice to *avoid them* is excessively feeble, and the criticism is over-compensated by fulsome praise of their *obedience* which *has spread everywhere*. Moreover, *the God of peace* (belatedly in mind, it would seem) crushing Satan beneath their feet is out of key with Paul's other references to the archaic title Satan. Elsewhere Satan is useful for dealing with immoral Christians and for keeping Paul humble (I Cor. 5.5; II Cor. 12.7); otherwise he is anything from a nuisance to a damned nuisance. He hinders apostolic plans and provides religious trickery for sham apostles; he can provoke resentment and lack of sexual control, indeed aggressive and destructive wickedness (I Thess. 2.18; II Cor. 11.14; 2.11; I Cor. 7.5; II Thess. 2.9). The imagery of trampling on evil spirits was known, in the popular Testaments of the Twelve Patriarchs, nearly two hundred years before Paul's day.

The best indication of what it means is a saying of Jesus: 'I have given you the power to tread underfoot snakes and scorpions and all the forces of the enemy. Nothing will ever harm you' (Luke 10.19). Be *expert in goodness, but innocent of evil, and the God of peace will* quickly (rather than *soon*) *crush Satan beneath your feet.* What is promised is an ever-present help in trouble, not an assurance that trouble will cease.

Greetings and doxology
16.21–27

16.21–23   The Epistle is Paul's creation: his active mind, his scriptural knowledge, his pharisaic training, his travelling experience and advocacy, his passionate apostolate of the Gentiles mark every page of it. But still he writes as belonging to a body of Christians: helped, supported, checked, and informed by others. So his companions send their greetings also. His *colleague Timothy* (joint-author with Paul of I and II Thessalonians, II Corinthians, and Philemon) whom he recruited at Lystra (40 kilometres south of Konya in the middle of modern Turkey), who played a large part in establishing and handling Christian development in northern and southern Greece (Acts 16–20; I Thess. 3.2, 6; I Cor. 16.10–11; II Cor. 1.19; Phil. 2.19–24). There were three fellow-Jews, and Tertius the letter writer – who may sometimes have struggled when he took down (no doubt in fairly short dictations) the Epistle that became one of the influential documents of Western culture. Also Paul's host Gaius, probably named in I Cor. 1.14, one of the few personally baptized by Paul, with a house large enough to accommodate the (still not very large) whole congregation of Corinth. Finally Erastus, the city treasurer, who may have been a high official but, even if not, he was on the inside of city administration. He is balanced by Quartus (a common name of slaves and freemen), notable by his membership of the Christian family.

16.25–27   On the missing verse 24, and the variable position of this doxology, see p. 123. The elaborate doxology was clearly intended as a summation of the Epistle. *Glory for endless ages* (so much for those who thought the end of all things was at hand!) is to be ascribed *through Jesus Christ to the only wise God who has power to make you stand firm*, as Paul had hoped at 1.11. (NRSV quite properly has 'strengthen' in both places.) The reverential language corresponds to similar ascriptions in I Tim. 1.17 and Jude 25, and is inherited from Judaism. Two hundred years earlier II Macc. 1.25 displayed the proper prayer style: 'You are the only Giver, the only just and omnipotent and eternal One.' To address God as 'only wise' conveys the faith that all his actions are well-informed, effective, and loving. But Paul might have said it differently: contrast I Cor. 1.25 where 'the folly of God is wiser than human wisdom'.

The ascription is to be made *according to* three basic convictions: (1) *My gospel* (the phrase he used at 2.16) *and the proclamation of Jesus Christ.* (2) *The revelation of that divine secret* (similarly in Eph. 3.3) *kept in silence for long ages* (nothing about such silence elsewhere in Paul, but the contemporary Jewish writing called Pseudo-Philo says that 'Darkness and silence were before the world was made, and silence spoke a word and the darkness became light' 60.2 – which is something like the beginning of John's Gospel; bishop Ignatius at the end of the first century effectively used silence imagery) *but now disclosed through prophetic scriptures* (there is a possibly illuminating parallel in II Peter 1.19). (3) *The eternal God's command* (a similar phrase in I Tim. 1.1 and Titus 1.3) *made known to all nations, to bring them to faith and obedience* (as at 1.5).

The doxology combines genuinely Pauline phrases and supplements them with expressions that became familiar later in the century. It is therefore good testimony that the post-Pauline church was willing to maintain Paul's theology and make it their own – an aim that has been modestly attempted in this commentary.

INDEX OF WORDS EXPLAINED IN THE TEXT